AVOIDANT ATTACHMENT

Why is your partner cold and detached in your relationship? Improve intimacy, emotional connection and understand why your dismissive partner behaves the way they do

DAVID LAWSON PHD

© **Copyright 2020 by David Lawson PhD - All rights reserved.**

The content contained within this book may not be reproduced, duplicated or transmitted without direct written permission from the author or the publisher.

Under no circumstances will any blame or legal responsibility be held against the publisher, or author, for any damages, reparation, or monetary loss due to the information contained within this book; either directly or indirectly.

Legal Notice:

This book is copyright protected. This book is only for personal use. You cannot amend, distribute, sell, use, quote or paraphrase any part, or the content within this book, without the consent of the author or publisher.

Disclaimer Notice:

Please note the information contained within this document is for educational and entertainment purposes only. All effort has been executed to present accurate, up-to-date, and reliable, complete information. No warranties of any kind are declared or implied. Readers acknowledge that the author is not engaging in the rendering of legal, financial, medical or professional advice.

TABLE OF CONTENTS

INTRODUCTION 1
PART 1: UNDERSTAND 3
CHAPTER 1 THE FOUR ATTACHMENT STYLES OF LOVE 4
   Secure Love Style 5
   Anxious Preoccupied Love Style 7
   Dismissive Avoidant Love Style 8
   Fearful Avoidant Love Style 10
CHAPTER 2 WHAT IS YOUR ATTACHMENT STYLE? (ATTACHMENT TEST) 12
   Directions 12
      Key 15
CHAPTER 3 IS AVOIDANT PERSONALITY DISORDER SERIOUS? ARE AVOIDANTS ABUSIVE? 19
PART 2 - WHEN YOU LOVE SOMEONE WITH A AVOIDANT ATTACHMENT STYLE 22
CHAPTER 4 WHAT ATTRACTS AVOIDANT PARTNERS IN RELATIONSHIPS—DO AVOIDANTS FEEL LOVE? . 23
CHAPTER 5 DATING SOMEONE WITH AN AVOIDANT ATTACHMENT STYLE 25
   Dating Someone with a Dismissive Avoidant Love Attachment Style 25
   Dating Someone with a Fearful Avoidant Attachment Style 29
CHAPTER 6 THE LOVE ADDICT & LOVE-AVOIDANT DYNAMIC 31
   Anxious Attachment Traits 31
   Avoidant Attachment Traits 31
CHAPTER 7 COMMUNICATION IN RELATIONSHIPS 33
   General Tips for Better Communication 33

- Active listening 33
- Open-ended questions 35
- Internal Editing 35
- Keep calm 36
- Being gentle 37
- Incorporate "I" statements 37
- Perspective 38
- Understanding 38
- How to Respond When Your Partner Is Evasive 39

CHAPTER 8 TOXIC RELATIONSHIP/WHEN IT'S TIME TO LEAVE A RELATIONSHIP 40

- Things You Should Know About Leaving a Toxic Relationship 40
  - It Takes Time for the Damage to Heal 40
  - You May Want to Go Back 41
  - The Decision Can Come from Anywhere 41
  - You May Not Understand What's Normal for Some Time 42
  - You May End Up in a Toxic Relationship Again 42
  - There can be Danger Associated with Toxic Relationships when Leaving 42
  - Leaving May Be the Best Decision for You 43
  - People May Not Understand Your Decision 43
  - Leaving a Toxic Partner Makes You Feel Good 44
  - Leaving a Toxic Relationship 44
- Getting Your Finances in Order 46
  - Think About What Brought You to This Position 48
  - Fall Back on Family and Friends 49
  - Make a Clean Break 49
  - Surround Yourself With Positive People 50
  - Do Not Feel Sorry for Yourself 50
  - Talk to a Therapist 51
  - Be Firm with Your Decision to Leave 51
  - Don't Forget to Love Yourself 52

CHAPTER 9 BEST STRATEGIES TO HELP YOUR AVOIDANT PARTNER 53

CHAPTER 10 COUPLES THERAPY EXERCISES 56

- A Healthy Relationship Makes Life Better 56
- Questions to Identify the Strengths and Weaknesses of Your Relationship 57
- Be in Love with Yourself 57
- Love is a Commitment More than a Feeling 58
- Investing in the Relationship 58
- Authentic Communication 59
- Admire Your Partner 60
- Change Yourself Rather than Changing your Partner 61
- Choose Your Arguments Wisely 62
- Power is Worth Sharing 62

PART 3: REWIRING YOUR AVOIDANT, DISMISSIVE, OR FEARFUL ATTACHMENT STYLE 64

CHAPTER 11 THE NEW SKILLS YOU NEED TO LEARN 65

- Communication Skills in a Love Relationship 65
- What Aspects Can We Improve When We Communicate in a Love Relationship? 65
- Practice Unconditional Acceptance 67
- Learn to Be With Yourself 68
- Learn to Be Alone 68
- Learn to Deactivate the Ego 69
- Is it Possible to Change the Attachment Pattern We Learn in Childhood? 70

CHAPTER 12 CHANGE YOUR INTERNAL WORKING MODEL 71

- Starting Points 71
- Five Starting Points for Working on Yourself 72
- Areas of Focus for Self-Work 73
- Family of Origin 73
- Inner Child Work 74
- Codependency/ Addiction Issues 74
- Self-Esteem 75
- Trauma 75
- The Good News, and the Bad 76
- Avoidant Attachment Style and Friendship 77
  - *Friendship for Dismissive Avoidant Personalities* 77

Friendship for Fearful Avoidant Personalities 78

CHAPTER 13 HOW TO FIND YOUR PARTNER 79
Building Healthy Relationships 80
- *Open Communication* 82
- *Overcoming Jealousy* 82
- *Emotional Connection Done Right* 83
- *Trust-Building Tips* 84

CHAPTER 14 HOW TO FEEL GOOD WITHOUT A RELATIONSHIP 85
- *Self-Assertion* 86
- *Being Your Own Best Friend* 87

Saying No to Toxic Relationships 89
Knowing Which Walls to Build 90
Tips for Building Better Boundaries 91
- *Identify your Limits* 91
- *Be Assertive* 91
- *Cultivate Self-Awareness* 92
- *Consider Your Unresolved Issues* 92
- *Prioritize Your Needs* 92

CHAPTER 15 HEAL YOUR ATTACHMENT WOUNDS .93
Self-Directed Healing 93
- *Allow Yourself to Grieve* 94
- *Make Sense of Your Story* 94
- *Find a Partner with a Secure Attachment Style* 95
- *Question Your Core Beliefs About Yourself* 96
- *Confront the Romantic Narrative* 97
- *Strengthen our Self-Compassion* 98
- *Pay Attention to Your Physical Body* 99
- *Working with a Therapist* 99
- *Psychoanalysis Therapy* 100
- *Cognitive Behavioral Therapy* 101
- *The Hoffman Process* 101
- *Hypnotherapy* 101
- *How to Find the Right Therapist* 102

CONCLUSION 104

INTRODUCTION

Regardless of whether single or in a relationship, numerous individuals accept that they'll never be happy in love. They feel neglected and need friendship—not only a pal to sit close to at a movie, but a friend, associate, and darling to go with them through that most prominent of all experiences we call life. They frequently fear that their partners will bolt once they become more acquainted with "the genuine me." Sometimes, they feel that their partners welcome the things they do. However, this isn't enough. There's the ever-present worry of whether anybody would really be there for them if they seek that individual for help, solace, and consolation. If you identify with any of these battles, then this book is the right one for you.

This book will help you understand the different attachment styles and recognize how avoidant attachment affects your relationship.

As with nearly everything else throughout everyday life, you find out about attachment relationships through understanding. Furthermore, since your first genuine relationship started as a baby with your guardians, that is the place you started finding out about relationships. I realize that is one of the adages of brain science, but at the same time, it's real. Your first exercises on how accessible and sustaining others will be the point at which you need them, and on how lovable you yourself are, depended on the glow, acknowledgment, and consolation offered by your folks or other people who raised you. During the early months and long stretches of your life, you built up a specific style of associating with—and connecting to—other people.

Understand that attachment-related anxiety doesn't need to be in light of any clearly damaging or destructive child-rearing; indeed, it frequently isn't. Several individuals with attachment-related anxiety originate from loving homes. Shockingly, their folks' own battles, difficult or horrendous conditions meddled with their ability to parent, despite the fact that they genuinely loved their kids.

One significant component in supporting self-awareness is to create more mindfulness. This incorporates monitoring your thoughts; recognizing and deliberately encountering your feelings, and understanding what is most important for you. This can be difficult, particularly when you are confronting disagreeable or clashing parts of yourself. Nonetheless, they give you a superior thankfulness for your battles. Such mindfulness, most of the time assists individuals with a more noteworthy feeling of prosperity and, without the help of anyone else, regularly encourages change, for example, lessening attachment-related anxiety as well as sustaining more beneficial relationships.

While the primary purpose of this book is to enable you to understand what you can do to discover the joy in a close attachment, the thoughts that I will present can likewise assist you with understanding your partner better.

In some cases, a window into your partner's reality helps you identify with that person more mercifully, which can assist you with nurturing a more beneficial relationship.

PART 1: UNDERSTAND

CHAPTER 1

THE FOUR ATTACHMENT STYLES OF LOVE

There are four different styles of attachment when it comes to a child's relationship with his or her primary caregiver. Our childhood attachment style can have far-reaching implications on the way we react to situations in later life.

One of the greatest facets of life affected by our childhood attachment styles is our ability to love and build romantic relationships.

Perhaps this is what drew you to this book. Maybe you always seem to attract partners with similar characteristics. Or perhaps you continually date people who don't turn out to be as compatible with you as you first thought.

But have you ever stopped to think about why you are attracted to the people you are?

Falling in love and building relationships involves constant choice, commitment, and work. While love can be extremely rewarding, and even exhilarating, it is often far from easy. Connecting with a romantic partner requires us to develop an understanding of the behavior of both our loved one and ourselves.

Researchers have determined that everyone has a certain **love style** based on their upbringing. A love style is constituted of our behaviors and inclinations with regards to how we respond to our romantic partners. By making sense of the way we love, we can learn how our love styles affect our relationships. Understanding our inclinations and tendencies in relationships can help us to make sense of our own—and our partner's—behavior, and build stronger, long-lasting relationships.

Secure Love Style

Those of us lucky enough to have a secure love attachment style have a significant advantage when it comes to finding partners and maintaining meaningful, loving relationships. People with a secure love style generally feel able to go to their partner with any issues or problems, allowing for meaningful, productive discussions. A secure love style also means you have great trust in your partner, allowing them the freedom to explore their own interests and pursue their own goals.

This leads to open, loving, and honest relationships in which both partners are equal. It provides an environment in which both parties can thrive, grow, and be happy.

Having a secure love style means we are comfortable having separate interests from our lover, but also understand how to mesh and work together to build a loving and secure partnership with which to go through life.

Maybe you're thinking this all sounds too good to be true. But it's important not to confuse a secure love style with perfection. Because, as we know, perfection is something unattainable, especially when it comes to love and relationships.

Having a secure attachment style does not mean we are immune from conflict, arguments, and bad days. Far from it. The nature of building a romantic relationship means there will always be disagreements. But where those with a secure attachment style differ is in their ability to work with their partner to problem solve, in order to reach an agreeable resolution to any conflict that may arise. Those with a secure attachment style also have higher emotional intelligence, which leads them to seek solutions, rather than acting rashly, striking out, or attacking their loved one.

Great resilience and self-awareness are typical characteristics of people with a secure love style—traits that assist them in moving past obstacles and conflicts maturely and lovingly. Secures have the capacity to reflect on their own emotional states, along with the emotional states of their partner. This allows them to communicate more effectively. As a result, secures perform well in partnerships and are able to respond appropriately to the emotional messages their loved one sends them.

Outside of romantic relationships, people with a secure attachment style make excellent colleagues, due to their ability to work well in teams. On average, they have higher incomes than those with insecure attachment styles.

Though we will look more closely at ways of assessing attachment style in the following chapter, if you can answer yes to most or all of these questions, you may exhibit a secure attachment style:

- Do you feel a strong emotional connection to the loved ones in your life?
- Are you comfortable with emotional and physical closeness?
- Are you equally comfortable with independence?
- Do you feel as though you communicate effectively?
- Do you have the ability to resolve conflicts when they arise?

- Do you feel as though the relationships in your life are fairly stable?
- Do you trust your partner?
- Do you feel comfortable opening up and being vulnerable around your partner?

Anxious Preoccupied Love Style

For people with an anxious preoccupied love style, love is often a thing relegated to the world of fantasy. They romanticize love and are prone to falling for a fantasy, or unobtainable ideal, as this is far easier to manage than the often-challenging reality of maintaining a relationship.

This romantic view of love often leads anxious preoccupied lovers to be attracted to partners who they perceive as "needing saving," or, conversely, partners they believe can save them. Anxious preoccupied lovers often find themselves seeking an unobtainable fairy-tale ending.

People with this attachment style often suffer from insecurities and self-doubt and struggle to find a strong sense of their own identity.

Whilst in a relationship, people with this attachment style can be clingy, demanding, and obsessive. They often overthink and overanalyze situations and can be moody and unpredictable. As a result, their relationships can be tempestuous and troubled, with anxious preoccupied lovers mistaking this constant conflict for passion.

Outside of romantic relationships, people with an anxious preoccupied attachment style are often dissatisfied with their jobs and have a lower income than those in a secure relationship.

If you answer yes to some or all of the following questions, you may exhibit an anxious preoccupied love style:

- When you argue with your loved one, does it make you feel extremely anxious and overwhelmed?
- When your partner requests a little alone time, do you hound them for attention until they give in?
- Do you feel the need for constant reassurance within your relationship?
- If your partner is away, does it make you question their love for you?

The anxious preoccupied love style is closely tied to the anxious ambivalent attachment style. Generally, those who exhibit one will also exhibit the other.

Dismissive Avoidant Love Style

A dismissive avoidant love style is characterized by being distant and detached in relationships. People with this attachment style often have strong personalities and come across as independent and self-sufficient.

But this strength is often just a cover for their inability to share feelings and express their emotions. People with this love style often withdraw at the first sign of conflict, cutting themselves off from any chance at true emotional intimacy.

It's important, of course, in any relationship, for both people to have personal space and time away from their partner. But those of us with a dismissive-avoidant love style will seek solitude far more often than most people. They will often push their partner away and deflect their advances, seeking the safety of their own personal space. In the eyes of someone with a dismissive-avoidant love style, spending time with a romantic partner puts them at risk of being vulnerable and getting hurt.

When a crisis hits a relationship, in the form of conflict, or even a breakup, people with this love style have the ability to close themselves off and convince themselves—at least for a while— that they don't care about what's happening. Their strong, independent personality kicks in, and they convince themselves they are happy on their own.

But this steely independence can only last so long. As humans, we need contact with others in order to survive. None of us can prosper on our own. The reality is that the steely façade portrayed by people with a dismissive-avoidant love style is just a front for a deep-seated lack of self-worth.

Those with a dismissive avoidant love style will avoid showing affection such as hugs, and will often avoid making eye contact.

A dismissive avoidant love style can manifest itself outside of romantic relationships too. People with this love style have difficulty maintaining close relationships of all kinds, whether with friends, family, or lovers.

The most extreme avoidants are almost entirely incapable of talking about their feelings. The feelings they do have are primarily negative, and they have great difficulty putting them into words. This is known as *alexithymia*—a syndrome referring to the inability to find words for feelings. It is important to note that this is not the same as *not having* feelings. Extreme avoidants suffering from alexithymia are often only able to express themselves through rage and tantrums. Their emotions can also manifest as physical symptoms such as unexplained stomach pains or rushes of adrenalin.

Outside of romantic relationships, people with an avoidant attachment style are prone to being workaholics. Letting work take over their life is often a ploy to avoid social situations. Avoidants generally prefer to work alone. Because of their work ethic, their incomes are often as high as those with a secure attachment style, but they are often just as dissatisfied with their jobs as anxious preoccupieds. However, their work ethic and ability to act alone makes people with avoidant personalities excel in roles that require individual effort. Their lack of empathy and concern for others' feelings can also be beneficial in fields such as litigation.

If you can answer yes to some or all of the following questions, you may exhibit a dismissive avoidant attachment style:

- Do you feel closest to your loved ones when you are apart?
- Do you find yourself pulling away when your partner is seeking emotional or physical intimacy?
- Do you seek to remove yourself from stressful situations of conflict?
- Do you feel emotionally disconnected from others?

The dismissive avoidant love style is most often exhibited by people with an anxious avoidant attachment style.

Fearful Avoidant Love Style

For people with a fearful avoidant love style, maintaining a relationship is something of a juggling act. They simultaneously fear being both too close and too distant from their partner. For those with fearful avoidant attachment issues, love can be akin to a terrifying roller-coaster ride.

Such people understand that, in order to build a strong relationship, they must allow themselves to get close to another person. But doing this makes them fearful, as they are scared of being abandoned. They struggle to build trust and rely on their partner and often have little confidence in the strength of their relationship.

Unsurprisingly, this leads them to behave unpredictably, and they can become overwhelmed by the intensity and inconsistency of their own emotions. People with this attachment style struggle with endless inner conflict: on the one hand, they crave intimacy, and on the other, they resist it, out of fear of getting hurt.

For fearful avoidant lovers, relationships are often full of highs and lows. They often find themselves clinging to their partner when they start to feel rejected, which, in some cases, can lead to emotionally and physically abusive relationships.

Just like with the dismissive avoidant love style, these traits can lead a person to have a few close friends and meaningful relationships in all facets of their life.

If you can answer yes to any of the following questions, you may exhibit a fearful avoidant attachment style:

- Do you desperate seek emotional intimacy, but simultaneously feel as though it's safer to be on your own?
- Do you feel like emotional or physical intimacy will lead to you getting hurt?
- As a child, was your primary caregiver physically or emotionally abusive?
- Did your primary caregiver show love one minute and hurt you the next?

The fearful-avoidant love style is most often exhibited by those with an anxious disorganized attachment style.

CHAPTER 2

WHAT IS YOUR ATTACHMENT STYLE? (ATTACHMENT TEST)

Directions

This quiz is designed to determine your attachment style. In the statements below, highlight the answers that sound most like yourself. Refer to the key to find your primary attachment style, along with other attachment style tendencies that exist within you.

1. I can be very emotionally present with others, but it takes me a while to share vulnerable things about myself.
2. I practice excellent care for both myself and my partner.
3. I often put my partner on a pedestal.
4. I easily feel irritated or impatient around my partner.
5. I feel comfortable around my partner and enjoy their company.
6. I have a strong desire for deep conversation in a romantic relationship.
7. I feel terribly upset when others infringe on my need for space or time alone.
8. I prefer not to spend much time alone.
9. I do not make whimsical decisions about leaving a relationship.

10. I tend to quite frequently be out of touch with my emotions.
11. I am very in tune with the needs of my partner and I notice when there is a change in behavior.
12. I express my emotions easily.
13. I constantly want to be emotionally closer to my partner.
14. I know how to process my emotions effectively when I feel upset.
15. I easily notice a change in people's micro-expressions, body language, and tone of voice.
16. I worry that my partner will fall out of love with me or eventually get bored of me.
17. I am effective at compromising and communicating.
18. I have extraordinarily strong emotions in relationships.
19. I strongly dislike feeling vulnerable around others.
20. If I notice my partner showing any signs of coldness, I panic and want to get closer as quickly as possible.
21. I do not hold grudges easily or keep resentments for long.
22. I often express anger very strongly when I feel hurt, powerless, or betrayed.
23. I do not feel as if there are any boundaries between myself and my romantic partner.
24. I feel as though conflict is resolvable and feel equipped to work through problems effectively.
25. It is not unusual for me to experience inward emotional turbulence throughout the duration of a romantic relationship.
26. I can be cold and standoffish when I do not know others very well.
27. I often feel extremely hot or very cold toward my partner or loved one.
28. I know that I am worthy of a healthy, happy relationship.

29. I usually wish that my partner would take care of their own emotions and needs and involve me less.
30. When I feel hurt, I often have thoughts about leaving the relationship immediately.
31. I do not feel as though I need anything from my romantic partner.
32. I am good at listening to other people's needs and expressing my own.
33. I often worry that my partner will reject me or pull away.
34. I do not enjoy being out of relationships.
35. If my partner's behavior hurts me, I will express my feelings and try to understand what caused them to act that way.
36. Relationships are often confusing or emotionally difficult for me.
37. I do not like making social plans with others in advance.
38. I sometimes feel as though I am constantly chasing my partner's love and affection.
39. I find it difficult to trust others in a romantic relationship and am often suspicious.
40. I find that setting boundaries comes naturally to me.
41. There have been times when I have threatened to leave the relationship and then changed my mind.
42. I often avoid conflict and feel very hurt by criticism.
43. I am not afraid of commitment, but I do not jump into relationships without assessing them first.
44. I am afraid that if I ask too much from my partner, they will leave me.
45. I focus much more on the relationships in my life than I do on myself.
46. I develop feelings easily but feel as if I am constantly doubting or questioning them as I get closer to my partner.

47. Sometimes the idea of commitment in a romantic relationship makes me feel afraid or invaded.
48. I often feel protective of my space, privacy, and belongings.
49. I am emotionally stable in my romantic relationships.
50. I tend to operate in extremes between being very emotionally available and then requiring time and space to myself.
51. I find it too easy to open up to people and sometimes overshare.
52. I do not express my emotions to others easily.
53. I do not tend to overshare, but I do not fear sharing my feelings with a partner.
54. I generally feel invaded when my partner demands too much physical affection.
55. I hunger for closeness, but often fear being truly vulnerable around my partner.
56. I find it much easier to process my emotions on my own than with others.
57. I would prefer to spend most of my free time with my partner.
58. I feel that it is easy to express my needs to my romantic partner.
59. I find that my partner usually emotionally recovers from a conflict before I do.
60. I deeply fear being abandoned by my partner.

KEY

FA = Fearful-Avoidant

DA = Dismissive-Avoidant

S = Secure

A = Anxious

1) FA
2) S
3) A
4) DA
5) S
6) FA
7) DA
8) A
9) S
10) DA
11) FA
12) A
13) A
14) S
15) FA
16) A
17) S
18) FA
19) DA
20) A
21) S
22) FA
23) A
24) S
25) FA
26) DA
27) FA
28) S
29) DA
30) FA
31) DA

32) S
33) A
34) A
35) S
36) FA
37) DA
38) A
39) FA
40) S
41) FA
42) DA
43) S
44) A
45) A
46) FA
47) DA
48) DA
49) S
50) FA
51) A
52) DA
53) S
54) DA
55) FA
56) DA
57) A
58) S
59) DA
60) A

Add up your results in each category using the key above. Remember, we are not a single attachment style. Your answers will provide you with your primary attachment style, along with the tendencies you share with other attachment styles.

Fearful-Avoidant (FA): _____

Dismissive-Avoidant (DA): _____

Secure (S): _____

Anxious (A): _____

Once you have determined your results from the quiz above, it is recommended that you take a closer look at the initial core wounds and attachment patterns explained above.

As you come to understand the interactions more deeply between your attachment style and the styles of your loved ones, you will be empowered to communicate more effectively. You will also be able to understand what your sensitivities are in relationships and what is likely to trigger your loved ones. You will then be provided with tools and strategies that will allow you to break through the limitations that might exist because of conflicting attachment dynamics.

It is important to remember that your attachment style results are not a diagnosis. These are simply a set of patterns that you have developed over time because of your experiences. These patterns can be changed with intention, or they may change because of exposure to new experiences. Through awareness of these patterns, you have a greater chance to thrive in your relationships.

CHAPTER 3

IS AVOIDANT PERSONALITY DISORDER SERIOUS?

ARE AVOIDANTS ABUSIVE?

For some people, the simple act of greeting another person can be traumatizing. Facing another person and risking being judged, criticized, or rejected is too much. Though this may be at the more extreme end of the problem, Avoidant Personality Disorder (or AvPD) makes situations exactly like this one a reality. AvPD patients are so focused on what other people think of them, that most decide to no longer interact with other people. This, in turn, can lead to a very lonely and depressing lifestyle, as well as a dangerous one. With the exponential growth of virtual communication, socialization, and interaction, there is both a higher probability as well as an easier way to hide a condition like AvPD. Utilizing the networks, gaming and social, that are available, it is quite easy and common for people to establish a persona very unlike who they are in reality. What results is a group of people with deeply established fears of other people and the acceptance of who they really are in person. This virtual interaction can both enable and hide mental disorders that can grow to be quite severe. Someone with AvPD could use online avatars, profiles, and game characters to create what they believe people will see as an acceptable personality. Though they know that the created persona is not their actual personality, they find it easier to interact through them. This then allows a bigger buildup of dislike and humiliation of themselves as they see each improvement of the false self as a reflection of the negative aspects of their true self. As confusing as it may seem, this is sometimes the only way people with Avoidant Personality Disorder can relate and interact with others without feeling the exaggerated pressures they find in face-to-face interactions.

Avoidant Personality Disorder can be broken into four subtypes: phobic, conflicted, hypersensitive, and self-deserting. Each subtype represents a more defined version of the illness and how it affects the patient. Phobic subtypes have a specific fear of something or someone in particular. Conflicted persons tend to find themselves consistently confused by the actions they are to take and the worry that stems from the fear of those actions. Hypersensitives are generally oversensitive to the reactions and information they get from other people or circumstances. Self-deserting is represented by the intentional withdrawing of one into themselves and the utilizing of a fantasy self as reality, even though this increases their perception of their own shortcomings in reality.

There are two possible speculations of what causes AvPD. One is genetic and the other is environmental. Genetics focus more on other symptoms that can actually result as a cause of AvPD, like anxiety or depression. Environment can cover anything from traumatic experiences to a neglected childhood. No one cause or definitive reasoning is yet to be fully established. Other conditions that can be attributed to AvPD are schizophrenia, severe depression, suicidal tendencies, bipolar disorder, multiple personality disorder, social anxiety disorder, a plethora of various phobias, and an overall avoidance of contact with people.

There is a wide range of symptoms of Avoidant Personality Disorder. The basis of AvPD is the underlying social anxiety disorder. Anxiety can lead to conflict that, in turn, leads to stress and further anxiety. This can result in fear, phobias, and depression. When the symptoms combine, it forms a person who is not able to function in cohesion with other people properly. Only in understanding the presence of the individual symptoms can the big picture lead to a diagnosis of Avoidant Personality Disorder.

There is a multitude of different therapies available for people with AvPD. The majority of therapies focus on helping the person understand their condition and the fact that they are the ones with the capability to change how they view things in order to overcome these hindrances. Medication is usually reserved for those who have an underlying depression or anxiety issue. For others, it is more pertinent to help them learn how to socialize with people, how to interact in groups, and how to perceive themselves in a better light.

Avoidant Personality Disorder is a battle within a person to overcome irrational beliefs and fears about themselves and about social interactions. You can still live out your life with AvPD but will find yourself extremely limited in many aspects. People who cannot find positive inspiration about their own image and how they appear to others will not be able to fully function around others. This can affect everything, from their family and love life to their work environment. Assumptions and fears will cripple them even with the simple idea of socializing. Targeting the initial causes, base issues, and the resulting adherences will allow a therapist or doctor to help the patient move on in life without the looming disorder being so present. Though, like any learned or overly practiced behavior, someone with such an ingrained belief is rarely going to be able to completely overcome how they feel about themselves and other people.

PART 2 - WHEN YOU LOVE SOMEONE WITH A AVOIDANT ATTACHMENT STYLE

CHAPTER 4

WHAT ATTRACTS AVOIDANT PARTNERS IN RELATIONSHIPS—DO AVOIDANTS FEEL LOVE?

Dismissive avoidants are the hard cases: convinced that love is a foolish notion designed to entrap the weak in the dependency they hate. But even the fearful avoidant tends to believe less in the possibilities of romantic love for the long term; often because their experience has been that it doesn't last and is inevitably disappointing—having rationalized their way into ending many relationships because their partner wasn't good enough, they start to think they are either very unlucky or there aren't any candidates up to their exacting standards. As a variety of self-fulfilling prophecies, their pessimism is justified. Avoidant people are more likely to believe that love either does not exist or is likely to disappear once a relationship is formed. Avoidant people find it harder to fall in love and many even doubt that such a state is possible outside of movies and romantic stories. Even within a long-term relationship, anxious people are more likely to sustain their "passion," whereas an avoidant attachment style is associated with experiencing less passion over time.

Subconsciously, dismissives do seek out the attachment, though consciously they tell themselves that they want sex or a convenient helpmate, their conscious attitude is that some of their practical and immediate needs will be filled by a compliant partner. They can be very charming and persuasive, and for the less experienced or the quick-to-attach anxious preoccupied, filling their needs can seem rewarding for a time. But the lack of real feeling and affection will show itself in unresponsiveness, and if pushed, passive-aggressive contempt, physical or verbal abuse. The dismissive wishes to have his needs met, but your needs are not very significant to him or her. Yet we know they are often somatically affected by separations and loss of loved ones; it's just that these feelings are repressed and denied at a conscious level. Does a dismissive love their partner? The answer may be "yes, but they don't know it."

The fearful avoidants consciously seek out relationships and know they want to be with someone but can't control the urge to escape when their partner gets really close to them; it increases their anxiety to be truly known. Since they have never experienced a feeling of safety when completely open and intimate with a partner, they tend to see love as a theoretical goal and a need, but their anxiety has kept them from really experiencing it. If they got very close to someone, they subconsciously believe that someone would hurt or abandon them—so they find a way to get away from them first.

Overall, then, attachment insecurity is associated with less constructive attitudes toward romantic love. Avoidant deactivating strategies seem to inhibit romantic and altruistic forms of love and favor game playing or practicality rather than romance. Consistent with this conclusion, R. W. Doherty, Hatfield, Thompson, and Choo (1994) found that more avoidant people scored lower on scales assessing passionate (erotic) and companionate (agapic) forms of love.

CHAPTER 5

DATING SOMEONE WITH AN AVOIDANT ATTACHMENT STYLE

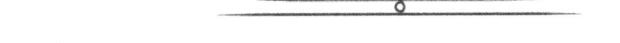

Dating Someone with a Dismissive Avoidant Love Attachment Style

Thanks to unreliable caregivers in childhood, people with a dismissive avoidant love style have a fear of intimacy and a belief that they do not need attachments. However, as these beliefs and fears are subconscious, you will likely still come across several dismissive avoidants in the dating pool.

The lack of love and security dismissive avoidants receive as children often lead to an inflated sense of self-importance. They have grown up with no one to rely on but themselves, which leads them to believe that they don't need anyone else in order to survive and succeed.

People with dismissive avoidant love styles pride themselves on their independence and self-sufficiency. They believe that needing others is a weakness and a trait that will hold them back. They can be distant, hostile, and condescending.

The dismissive avoidant has a tendency to end relationships without giving them a "real go." Often, they will hold an ideal in their mind of a previous relationship; an ideal to which they believe no one can ever measure up to. And when your relationship does end, the dismissive avoidant will act aloof, thanks to their belief that they are fine on their own.

In order to cultivate their protective shield of independence, dismissive avoidants often hate being asked to look inwards and examine their behavior, both past and present. They will often struggle to remember their childhood, having repressed the negative memories that led to the formation of their dismissive behavior. When they do recall attachment issues from their past, they often do so in a flippant or dismissive way, believing attachment is unimportant. They carry the belief that any negative experience—such as physical or emotional abuse from their parents—simply helped them become the strong, resilient person they are today.

The more you ask for attention and closeness, the more dismissive your partner will likely become. But of course, as humans, even dismissive avoidants have a biological need for connection. And when they are starved of this, they will engage in unhealthy behavior in order to compensate. For example, single dismissive avoidants may become workaholics, or obsessed with hobbies or sports. In relationships, being separated from their partner for an extended period of time may elicit similar behavior, only to have them act distant and hostile on their partner's return.

Dismissive avoidants will often seek to fulfill their biological needs for emotional and physical connection from less demanding partners—often anxious preoccupied lovers who require constant attention, regardless of whether it is based on real intimacy and connection.

If you find yourself dating someone with a dismissive avoidant attachment style, you will likely find them charming at first. They know well what is expected of them when dating and can play the role perfectly at first. But dismissive avoidants' view subconsciously sees being attached to others as a negative thing. They compare all new relationships to that unattainable ideal and are prone to quickly dismissing new relationships when they become inconvenient or time-consuming.

If the relationship does continue, dismissive avoidants will find faults in you and, contrary to the behavior of the anxious preoccupied, will focus only on your negative traits and shortcomings. But dismissive avoidants will go to great lengths to avoid talking about their feelings. The first clue you have that something is wrong may well be when your dismissive partner breaks up with you.

But if you experience this, it is important to realize that you are not to blame. A dismissive avoidant's upbringing renders them incapable of tolerating real intimacy, and when anyone tries to get close to them, their knee-jerk response is to run away. While outwardly, the dismissive avoidant may seek to blame others for his or her relationship failures, the reality is that, at their core, his or her self-esteem is so low they do not believe themselves worthy of love and affection. If you succeed in breaking through a dismissive avoidant's defensive shield, catching a glimpse of their insecurities beneath, they will panic and run, seeking either solitude or someone who does not realize they are not exactly what they seem.

In relationships, dismissive avoidant people engage in protective behavior known as "distancing," in order to keep their partners from getting too close. These behaviors include:

- Not returning phone calls or messages
- Telling their partner they are not ready to commit, but staying together anyway
- Focusing on their partner's flaws
- Comparing their partner to their ex

- Flirting with others to introduce insecurity into the relationship
- Refusing to say "I love you."
- Pulling away after positive interactions. (For example, not calling after a great date.)
- Forming relationships that do not have a future, such as with someone who is married.
- Avoiding sex
- Not wanting to share a bed with their partner

So, what should you do if you find yourself dating someone with a dismissive avoidant attachment style? While this attachment style can lead to potentially destructive and hurtful relationships, the first step in building a healthy relationship is understanding that this avoidant behavior is not your fault. Understand that it comes from your partner's deep-seated beliefs that began to take root in the very first years of their life.

Firstly, understand that anger or throwing a tantrum might be the only way a dismissive avoidant is able to communicate his or her feelings. It may be tempting for you to respond with anger of your own. But this will only add fuel to the fire. Instead of engaging with this negative behavior, take a step back. Walk away if you need to and return to the issue when you feel you can operate with a clear head and a calm state of mind. Express your needs in an adult way, without making demands or issuing ultimatums. After all, this is a sure-fire to get a dismissive avoidant to run in the opposite direction!

Do your best to calmly come up with solutions to the conflict that will benefit you both. For example, perhaps you're angry that your avoidant partner has failed to return your messages for three days straight. Instead of attacking him or her, understand that this is simply a characteristic of their attachment style and is not intended to hurt you. Ask that the next time he or she feels the need for space, they agree to let you know and to contact you the following day. This way, your partner will have the space they need, and you will not feel as though the relationship is being threatened.

People with dismissive avoidant attachment styles have a tendency to overthink things and get lost in their heads. To overcome this, it can be helpful to have dates that involve physical activity, such as hiking, playing a sport, or going dancing. The physical exertion will cause your partner to get out of their head and be present at the moment, and they will be more likely to connect and form a lasting bond.

Having an avoidant partner requires patience. While you may logically see that opening up and sharing their feelings will be beneficial, understand that this process does not come easily to people with an avoidant attachment style. Allow them personal space when they need it and be sure to be engaged and present when they are finally ready to share. The other key thing to remember is that for many avoidants, learning to share their feelings can be as simple as just naming their emotion. By encouraging this simple step, it can open the door to greater connection and openness.

Though they may not always act like it, the reality is that dismissive avoidants want – and need – love just as much as the rest of us. For dismissive avoidants to cultivate a healthy relationship, it is essential that they learn to open up and share with their partner.

Dating Someone with a Fearful Avoidant Attachment Style

Just like dismissive avoidants, fearful avoidant attachment styles come from a deep distrust of a person's caregiver. Because of the similarities between these two attachment styles, dating a fearful avoidant can be a similar experience to dating someone with a dismissive avoidant attachment style. Unlike dismissive avoidants; however, people with a fearful avoidant attachment style do not have the defensive shield of high self-esteem. They accept that they both want and need intimacy and attachment in their life.

Problems can arise, however, as the relationship develops. Fearful avoidants crave intimacy, leading them to get closer to their partner. But when they do, their old fears kick in, and they suddenly feel the need to pull away. This can lead to an endless series of short relationships, in which the fearful-avoidant seeks closeness, only to flee when they actually receive it.

In the dating pool, fearful avoidants often put on a façade; a front they believe makes them more likable. They can maintain this "false self" even in moments of intimacy. Just like dismissive avoidants, fearful avoidants have difficulty sharing their feelings with their partners. They are also characterized by weakened empathy, meaning they are often difficult to communicate with.

Dating someone with a fearful avoidant attachment style has many similarities with a dismissive avoidant partner.

If you find yourself dating someone with a fearful avoidant personality, once again, understand that their behavior is not a reflection of you. Their trait stems from the damaging belief that they are not worthy of love and affection.

CHAPTER 6

THE LOVE ADDICT & LOVE-AVOIDANT DYNAMIC

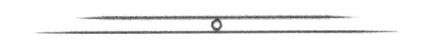

Anxious Attachment Traits

First, let's consider the traits and behaviors common amongst anxiously attached individuals. Anxiously attached people:

- Are sensitive to what their partner is thinking and feeling
- Always looking for signs of a partner's rejection
- Experience emotions such as fear, abandonment, anxiety, depression
- Act out and later regret behaviors
- Use manipulation to try and control the reaction/action of their partner
- Want to be very close with a partner
- Are fearful and insecure, and feel like they are flawed
- Become attached quickly, possibly even from afar

Avoidant Attachment Traits

Now, let's look at the general traits of avoidantly attached individuals. If you went the extra mile and made a list of characteristics of your current or former partners, it may be helpful to get it out and look at it. Otherwise, keep some of those relationships in the back of your mind and compare some of those people to the traits below.

- Do not want to be trapped by a relationship
- Do not discuss feelings or ask for support
- Pull people in, then push them away when too close
- Keep an escape route open
- Not outwardly worried about the relationship or seem bothered by its ups and downs
- Uncomfortable with intimacy
- Value being independent; view dependency as a weakness
- Blame their partners, not themselves, for issues in the relationship
- Move on from relationships quickly and without much emotional distress

How many of these traits can you recognize in your previous partners? Did it always feel like you were more invested than they were? That they were there but not really there? Some avoidants stay out of relationships or have a string of short flings, but other avoidants manage to be in a relationship for years, but never fully commit to their partner. Either way, their basic feeling is the same; deep down, they do want to be close to someone, but it makes them so uncomfortable that they do all that they can to be distant and not really present in a relationship.

CHAPTER 7

COMMUNICATION IN RELATIONSHIPS

Regardless of whether it is a relationship with your better half or even your friends, there will be some challenges. There are different factors that are important for the success of a partnership or even a long-term relationship. However, the most important factor of all is communication. The lack of proper communication skills can effectively ruin any relationship. It is quite important to effectively and efficiently communicate what you want, need, feel, or desire with your partner for the health of your relationship. The lack of proper communication often creates misunderstandings and feelings of resentment. These things can quickly ruin your relationship. Well, the good news is, as with any other skill in life, you can also work on improving your communication skills.

So, are you interested in learning about ways in which you can significantly improve the way you communicate with your partner?

General Tips for Better Communication

Active listening

There is a difference between hearing what the other person says, and actively listening to them. At times, you might even listen to what your partner says, but you may not be fully present while doing so. You might be distracted with something else. In regular conversations and especially during any heated conversations, you might impatiently wait to express your thoughts or wait for your chance of a rebuttal. You might be impatiently thinking about all the various ways in which you can respond to them while they are still speaking instead of actively soaking up what they are saying and then responding later. When you do this, you are not paying much attention to what your partner is saying because you're engrossed in your own thoughts.

In order to be an active listener, you must make a conscious effort to slow down your thoughts and listen to what your partner is saying, not just with an open mind, but with an open heart as well. Like most things in life, this is easier said than done. However, your intention is what matters, so this will be a starting point. If for some reason, you don't have the concentration to listen actively and openly to what others say, then you can put the argument or conversation on hold until later. Another simple way to work on becoming an active listener is by sharing your feedback. You merely need to restate or paraphrase whatever your partner says toward the end of the conversation to demonstrate the fact that you have been listening.

The dynamic of the conversation can shift in a positive manner when your partner knows that they are being seen and heard. That said, I'm not suggesting you have to agree with everything they say, but by showing that you understand them, you can effectively improve the communication in your favor. Even if you sound a little transparent while doing this, it is fine. At least you are making an effort to get started. For instance, you can say something like, "… did I understand this correctly?" Or "it seems like you are upset with me for not doing…"

As with any other skill in life, you can become an active listener, but it takes time and effort. The more practice you get, the better you will be, and the easier it will be for you. During the initial couple of weeks, active listening might not come naturally to you, but after a while, you will get the hang of it.

Open-ended questions

"Do you ever stop talking and ever listen?" or "I wonder if you will ever clean up without me asking?" You might have used such rhetorical questions at some point or other with your partner. Well, do these seem like great conversation starters to you? I'm sure even you would agree that this is not the best way to start a healthy conversation or a dialogue. Sure, when you are frustrated, upset, or annoyed, these might seem like pretty good things to say in that instance. However, these are not good for you in the long run. By making such statements or asking such questions, you are essentially putting your partner on the defensive once again. Once this happens, the scope for healthy discussion goes down the drain. Instead of transferring any unpleasant emotion into the conversation, start using open-ended questions. Instead of : "I wonder if you will ever clean up without me asking!" you can say something like, "I could certainly use more help around the house. What can we do about it?" or "It would be nice to get this all cleaned up quickly. What can we do?"

Internal Editing

While you are communicating with your partner, you must make a conscious effort to avoid resorting to any form of personal criticism. This means you must refrain from displaying criticism either verbally or through your body language. So, don't resort to any putdowns, insults, negative criticism, or display undesirable body languages such as eye-rolling or dramatic sighs. The minute you start being critical of your partner, you are immediately shifting into the defensive. Once your partner gets defensive, whatever the topic of conversation was, it is most likely to turn into an argument or a nasty fight. When you put your partner on the defensive, it significantly harms the entire conversation. It not only limits how much you listen, but the conversation will escalate out of anger, and you might both end up hurting each other with the things you say.

Keep calm

Whenever you are engrossed in discussion with your partner, ensure that you keep calm. If you stay calm, the chances of a conversation spiraling out of control and turning into a massive argument will decrease. If you want, you can take a break from the conversation and then revisit the issue when you feel more emotionally stable and calm. Encourage your partner to do the same. It is better to have a discussion when you and your partner are emotionally stable and not volatile. Also, you must become conscious of any internal self-talk going on in your mind while having a conversation with your partner. For instance, let us assume that you are in the middle of a disagreement. Does your internal self-talk increase your ability to calm yourself down, or does it make you even more irritated? If you notice that this internal self-talk seems to be fueling the fires of emotional distress, it is time to change it. While in the middle of an argument, if you catch yourself thinking, "the last time we had a fight, the things they said hurt me," or "this is what they always do, and it is unfair," then stop yourself immediately. Engaging in negative self-talk will only worsen the situation at hand. Don't do this and, instead, try to replace all this behavior with calmness. Once you are calm and are no longer seeing red, you are in a better position to express yourself and understand your partner.

Work on self-soothing whenever you are upset. For instance, maybe you can go for a short walk, or even take a timeout and physically remove yourself from the room your partner is in. This helps ensure that your emotions are in check, and you're the one in control of them. A conversation will be quite productive when your emotions are balanced, and your mind is clear.

Being gentle

If something bothers you, you are free to state the reasons for this. But while doing this, you must be gentle with your partner. Don't blame your partner, but instead talk about what you feel and have experienced. Be conscious of the tone you are using whenever you're communicating your problems. By using a tone that is mutually respectful, you can start a constructive dialogue and open up lines of communication between you both. Keep in mind that the tone you use must not be aggressive or passive. Once again, if your partner detects any hints of criticism or passive-aggressiveness, the entire conversation will come to a startling halt.

Incorporate "I" statements

The best way to own your feelings while communicating with your partner is by using "I" statements. Instead of pointing out your partner's mistakes, concentrate on expressing how you feel because of their actions. The most common phrases you can start using are, "I feel," "I want," or "I need." For instance, saying something like, "I feel bad that you said ___." By doing this, you are effectively preventing your partner from becoming defensive while expressing yourself. It will also make your partner more self-aware of their behavior. This technique also encourages you to express yourself, your thoughts and emotions, more clearly.

Perspective

Your perspective essentially determines everything you feel and think. For instance, you might say that the glass is half empty, while your partner says the glass is half full. Regardless of what you both think, the amount of water in the glass will stay the same. So, why not think this is true from your partner's perspective? After all, the content of liquid is the same, and your partner isn't wrong. By placing yourself in your partner's shoes in any situation, it becomes easier for you to view things from their perspective. Once you understand where they're coming from and why they are saying what they say, it becomes easier to understand them. It can also trigger feelings of empathy for you. The extent to which your relationship can be successful depends on whether you can accept influence from your partner or not. At times, all it takes is a mere shift in perspective to resolve a dispute.

Understanding

We all want to be understood, but one thing we all fail to do is understand others. You must first try to understand what the other person is saying before you demand that you are understood. This is a simple technique you can use while engaging in conversations with your partner, family members, friends, colleagues, or pretty much anyone in your life. As human beings, it is an inherent tendency or desire to be understood by others. Take a moment and think about all the times you've said, "No one understands me," or "You don't understand what I'm trying to say!" For a healthy, loving, and successful relationship, you and your partner must understand each other. For a moment, don't emphasize your need to be understood, and instead, shift the focus to understand them better. This simple shift in the way you use your attention helps clear a path for fresh communication and will cause a positive shift in the dynamic of the relationship.

How to Respond When Your Partner Is Evasive

As with every shift at such a deep level, understanding is the first move. You understand that you have an evasive approach, and you know it because of your partner's experiences.

Try to work for mutual cooperation and encouragement. Try to reduce the desire for full control. Enable your partner to do some things that are hard for you to do.

Don't always dwell on your partner's imperfections. We all have them.

Create a list of the things about your partner for which you are grateful.

Get used to considering and even instigating physical touch. Tell yourself that having some intimacy is good for you. Intimacy will help you to feel comfortable.

And you can learn over time that it's all right to rely on other people.

CHAPTER 8

TOXIC RELATIONSHIP/WHEN IT'S TIME TO LEAVE A RELATIONSHIP

Things You Should Know About Leaving a Toxic Relationship

Before you take the decisive step of leaving a toxic relationship, there are a few things you need to know. Knowing them will ensure the breakup process is much easier for you, so you are not caught unawares.

It Takes Time for the Damage to Heal

If you've been in a toxic relationship for a long time, it can be tough for you to love yourself. Due to the consistent emotional and physical abuse you've been through, you believe you're at fault and hate yourself for this. Your partner may have told you why you need help, maybe saying that you're emotionally unstable and crazy. After hearing it for so long, you believe this with time. This may have taken away your self-worth, and no matter what you do, you'll always remember these things. In the end, when you're ready to move on and let go, you'll begin to love yourself and gradually forget about them.

You May Want to Go Back

Toxic partners are excellent manipulators. They know your weaknesses and what you want. They'll ensure that you think about them wherever you are by treating you with love and kindness at the beginning of your relationship. Even if you have left them for a while, you still remember the romantic moments you shared, and you're tempted to go back. And even worse, you may feel ashamed for feeling this way. Nonetheless, you have to know that it's okay to feel this way, but if you give it time, you'll heal completely.

The Decision Can Come from Anywhere

It can be tough to spot unhealthy behaviors in your relationship after spending years in it. For this reason, you may not be the one to trigger the decision to break up. Your friends and loved ones are likely not going to be happy seeing you suffer, and they may make a recommendation, but you're not sure it's right. You may not understand what others are seeing because you're blindfolded by love.

Even in a situation where you are getting prepared to end the relationship, you may believe that the other individuals in your life are being too dramatic or blowing things out of proportion. You may also see the truth in what they are trying to tell you. However, with continuous pressure from them, you may end up making the decision to leave anyway. The decision to leave can be triggered from any location. This is not important. What is essential is that you do make the decision.

You May Not Understand What's Normal for Some Time

Due to the kind of environment you have grown accustomed to in your toxic relationship, you will believe that arguments and violence are a normal part of a relationship. You only get to understand what normal behavior is when you talk to your family, friends, and therapist. This process may take time, but eventually, you will understand. Toxic individuals continuously try to teach you the wrong definition of what is normal but having the right set of people in your life can show you what normal really is.

You May End Up in a Toxic Relationship Again

Leaving a toxic relationship and ending up in another can be very devastating. But there is a high chance that it will happen. There are numerous toxic individuals in this world, and you may come across one or more of them as you try to move on. In our quest to find happiness again, we should try as much as we can to heal completely and recognize toxic behaviors to prevent the repetition of events. This is because the individuals who tend to fall into toxic relationships again after leaving one are those who don't take time to learn, readjust, and recover. When we truly understand what toxicity means and what we should expect from healthy relationships, then we know how to avoid them.

There can be Danger Associated with Toxic Relationships when Leaving

Any partner that can abuse you emotionally can get physical, even if this is not usually the case. Some toxic partners are good at emotional abuse, while some can go as far as being physically violent. Some may have a weapon at their disposal and react in a terrifying way whenever you want to leave. You need to be watchful and smart. If a violent, toxic partner finds out you want to break up with them, they may lose it and try to cause you harm.

So, keep yourself safe by seeking out help if you can. Do this by letting your friends and family know before you take a step, or call the police. And if you know you are dealing with an extraordinarily violent partner, break up in an open environment and walk away forever. Regardless of the option you choose to go with, ensure your safety is a priority when trying to leave.

Leaving May Be the Best Decision for You

Leaving a toxic relationship can change your life completely. You'll have the opportunity to work on being a better you and discover your passion. You're able to live a life of peace, happiness, and love. Even though you'll feel the pain sometimes, it's only a part of your healing process, and you'll get past it.

In fact, you may not appreciate the fact that you left the toxic life behind until years after you left. By this time, you'll be able to find love again, and you'll be unstoppable.

People May Not Understand Your Decision

A toxic relationship is difficult to explain to people who haven't experienced it. These people may not understand why you are leaving and will not support your decision. Manipulative toxic partners often understand how to make themselves look good in the eyes of outsiders, especially friends and loved ones. For many people, your relationship is a perfect one that everyone idealizes. This makes it understandable that many won't understand your reasons for leaving.

Tell them everything without leaving anything out. If they aren't ready to listen, leave them with the hope that they will understand your reason for leaving years later. Remember that you are the one who knows where it hurts, so you need to think about yourself and your sanity before anyone else's.

Leaving a Toxic Partner Makes You Feel Good

You will experience an aura of freshness that comes with leaving toxicity. Never again will you have to watch your steps because you are scared of making your partner angry. You will be free from all the bullying and name calling. You will also be able to do anything you want without fear of judgment from the one you love. Just feel good and be happy! Close your eyes and embrace the feeling of the freshness of the air. You deserve to be happy, so you should be.

Now that you understand some of the difficulties you may face; let us break down the steps involved in leaving a toxic relationship for good.

Leaving a Toxic Relationship

Leaving a toxic relationship is not easy, and if you happen to be in one, remember that it is not your fault. However, as we have earlier stated, it is possible to leave, and the benefits that come along with leaving are enormous. You get to enjoy a life of freedom according to your rules, in an environment without manipulation and abuse.

There are a few practical steps you need to put in place beforehand, to make the process of leaving less complicated and more secure.

- ***Put a Safety Plan in Place***: When leaving a toxic relationship, especially one which involves abuse, it is crucial to plan for your safety. This becomes essential because you never can tell how a scorned toxic partner might react when you leave. Many of them are not predictable, and even if you feel like it is not a necessity, this is something that you should not overlook. For many victims of toxic relationships, one of the most dangerous periods is when they choose to leave. Let your safety be your priority. Create a plan with a professional or someone close to you.

- *Arrange for a Private and Secure Place to Reside:* This is still a part of staying safe. You need a secure location to stay that is unknown by your toxic partner. This becomes even more necessary if there are kids in the equation. The location could be with a loved one, friend, or a shelter for domestic violence sufferers. To ensure your chosen location stays confidential, it's best to keep your plans to yourself and just a few trustworthy family members. In a bid to help, lots of loved ones who have your best interest in mind may unknowingly divulge this information to your toxic partner. Many may not understand how serious the issue is, and may try to fix it in their way. In the end, the results can be more detrimental than positive.

- *Keep a Record of Everything:* Many toxic partners try to reach out to their victims in a bid to get them back. In the process, they may resort to threats, abuse, and manipulation. Do your best to restrict the way you communicate with your ex after he's gone. Ensure you keep a record of all the conversations you have. Take note of the time and dates. All of these will be vital if you ever get into a custody battle for your kids, which is a strategy commonly used by many toxic partners.

- *File for a Restraining Order if Required*: This is not a perfect option, however, a restraining order can deter many

toxic partners, especially physical abusers. It is also a great way to have the experiences you have had with your toxic partner on record. This kind of record can be useful if the matter does head to court.
- **Get Help with Childcare if There are Kids Involved:** Uprooting your life with kids can be difficult. However, having support can be a huge benefit. Regardless of whether you get help from a friend, babysitter, or daycare, ensure there is always someone you can call on in the event of an emergency. There may be things that might require your attention, which may be impossible to attend to if you are the only one looking after your kids.

Getting Your Finances in Order

A strategy commonly used by many toxic partners is to abuse their victims financially. They are quick to close shared accounts or ensure the victim has no access to funds if the need arises. This ensures that the victim is directly under their control. Due to this, it becomes crucial to have some form of financial backup away from your partner before you leave.

Below, we will cover a few ways you can achieve this:

- **Save and Save Even More**: Before you take the step to leave, be sure that you have some funds in your account. This account should be solely in your name and not in a joint account with your partner. Also, it can be helpful to get some credit cards that belong to you alone. All of these can come in handy if you need to leave in a hurry.

If you can, access a loan. It is an excellent option because your partner does not need to know about it or have access to it. You can get loans from family, friends, and other secure sources. Also, look out for other means of making cash that your partner will have no access to or information about.

Better still, if you have a paying job, you can reach out to your HR department to send a portion of your paycheck automatically to another account. It is also possible for your HR to help you alter your W-4, so you can get more cash invested or saved with every paycheck. There are numerous ways to get money you can save, and all you need to do is look for an option that suits you best.

- *Make Copies of Vital Documents*: Make copies of all documents related to your finance. These could range from your vehicle titles, bank statements, tax returns, loan information, and investment statements, among others. You can use a scanner to make virtual copies and save them on the cloud or a Google drive. Ensure you do this in a drive that only you have access to. This way, you can get copies of these documents anywhere in the world you decide to go.
- *Create a New Bank Account*: Open a new bank account that your partner is not aware of. To do this, you will require a new email and mailing address which your toxic partner has no information about. If your partner knows your previous account and has access to it, a great option will be to reach out to your bank and alter your security questions. It is possible to use a question only you know the answer to and doing this will make sure that only you have access to this account.

Furthermore, take out all of your private items from any deposit box you both used. Head to another bank and make a deposit box of your own. Here, you can place every vital document and valuable which can come in handy later on.

- ***Engage the Services of a Financial Advisor:*** If it is possible, engage the help of a licensed financial advisor, who can cater to your needs alone. They can encourage you during your downtimes. If you don't have the resources to hire an expert, there are literature and financial classes you can take advantage of at your local library.

Even friends and members of your family who are great at finance can be of assistance. Regardless of where you find yourself, there is most certainly someone who is very experienced in topics around money. This could be your co-worker, family member, or a loved one. Find a way to contact them and get the help you require.

After putting everything you require in place, the following are a few more steps that can ensure that leaving your toxic relationship is less complicated:

Think About What Brought You to This Position

One of the first things to do when you're trying to leave an unhealthy relationship is to think deeply about why you were attracted to the person and why you stayed. If you're able to provide an answer to this, you're one step away from leaving this person. This is because you will learn to point out the unhealthy behavior that makes your relationship toxic.

If you don't understand this, you may be tempted to go back because you won't understand why your relationship is toxic. Besides, learning to do this can be of benefit to you in the future. You'll be able to identify a toxic relationship without spending too much time in one. Any form of abuse, be it physical, emotional, or sexual, should not be tolerated in any relationship. You need to seek help, and there are lots of resources available online which you can leverage.

Fall Back on Family and Friends

When you're in situations that are beyond your control, your family and close friends are there for you. You can always reach out to them and let them know what's going on. They've got your back and will always want the best for you. Lean on them at this critical moment and ask for advice. If you think it's important, ask them for accommodation.

As a result of the time you've spent in an unhealthy relationship, you may find it hard to recognize the toxic behaviors or words that your partner uses on you. Your friends and family will help you see this if you open up to them without covering up for your partner. They'll be frank with you and let you see things the right way.

As soon as you notice red flags in your relationship, talk about it with a friend or family. You can speak to them in private and hear what they have to say. You may have failed to recognize the signs and looming danger, but your friends will help you see this. However, due to the vital role that family and friends play in our lives and the amount of support they provide us, a toxic partner will try to take you away from your loved ones or ensure you don't see or visit them as often as you should. If you find yourself in this situation, it's hazardous, and you should contact someone you trust immediately. Let them know about your partner's constant abuse and controlling habits. Doing this will make you happy, and you'll feel safe knowing that someone is aware of your partner's gameplay.

Make a Clean Break

Ensure that the breakup is as clean as possible. Be assertive and make your partner understand that there shouldn't be any contact between you. Tell them you will not tolerate being harassed or abused and will take legal action if they try that.

Stop feeling guilty or concerned about hurting their feelings. They do not care about your feelings, so why should you care about theirs? Right now, the only person important to you is YOU. Your happiness is more important than anyone's at this stage. So, make it a clean break to prevent them from coming back to you.

When people end unhealthy relationships, they're usually concerned about their safety, as the partner may abuse, harass, or even become violent with them. When you make a clean break, the probability of facing such issues becomes difficult. If you think your life is under threat and you aren't so sure about your partner's next line of action, involve the police.

Surround Yourself With Positive People

When you're leaving a toxic relationship, do not engage with negative people. Surround yourself with people that want the best for you. Practice self-love to attract people that'll treat you with love and care. Be positive and treat yourself well. Take yourself out on a date, spend time outdoors, exercise, go sightseeing, or do something that makes you happy. The time people spend in an unhealthy relationship is usually filled with stress and negativity. Replace these stressful and negative emotions with positive ones.

Do Not Feel Sorry for Yourself

Toxic relationships have the capacity to mess with our minds in the strangest ways, which is why they are so difficult to let go of. For one, you will find yourself feeling some self-pity, and the thought of moving on may weigh you down. You will also be full of anxiety and fear of letting go. It's okay to feel this way, but you shouldn't let this last for too long. As soon as these thoughts come to your mind, tell yourself that you're stronger than this and that moving on is for the best. Moving on will make you happy, and it's the best thing to do.

Talk to a Therapist

You might have considered talking to your family, but you're not so sure about their sense of judgment, or they just aren't a good option. Thus, the next step is to see a therapist or a third-party professional. Having someone to support you and look at your relationship from the perspective of an outsider is an excellent idea as they may give you cogent reasons to leave. They'll also speak to you frankly without being sentimental. Staying in a toxic relationship can affect your mental and physical health. In a research study carried out in 2014, it was discovered that people in unhealthy relationships have anxiety problems, disturbed sleep, heart problems, and stress. (Medic, Wille & Hemels, 2017)

After leaving a toxic relationship, these issues will always remain for the early part of your breakup until you're ready to let go and heal completely. It's just like getting healed from a physical wound.

Be Firm with Your Decision to Leave

Often, we miss people when we leave them, and this is normal. The bad parts of our relationships are usually forgotten while the good parts are most remembered. There are even times that we wish the person was still in our lives as we can't deal with their absence. This is why we need to engage in deep thought before making our decision.

You need to be sure that you're ready to do this and try as much as you can to stick to your decision. Always remind yourself of what you stand to gain by leaving and why it's the best option for you. If you find yourself unable to handle it alone, confide in your therapist, a close friend, or family. Let them know what you're thinking and why you need them now more than ever. They're there to provide the support you need, but you need to remain firm and stick to your decision.

Don't Forget to Love Yourself

Loving yourself is most important to you at this point, and you shouldn't compromise this for anything. Your happiness should come first in all you do. You don't even have to speak to the person you broke up with again if they aren't worth it. It's your happiness that matters, and you should associate yourself with only what makes you happy.

You can't find love in an unhealthy relationship, so, leaving such a relationship means you love yourself and you're putting yourself first. Sometimes, loving yourself comes from letting go. Instead of holding on to a relationship that clearly isn't working, spend time doing things you love. So, love yourself, and you'll start attracting happier and healthier relationships.

CHAPTER 9

BEST STRATEGIES TO HELP YOUR AVOIDANT PARTNER

For people with avoidant attachment, relying on someone too much can evoke panic and discomfort. For them, this discomfort can range from just a bit of stress to a full-blown threat response. Many types of interpersonal engagement, especially of an intense nature, can set off avoidant tendencies. As a friend, partner, collaborator, or family member of someone who gets triggered in this way, what can you do?

The first thing is to take the person's need for safety and comfort seriously. Taking the risk to engage in emotionally charged situations, even if they may seem simple to *you*, is not easy for people with avoidant attachment. For them, staying engaged in the conversation about an emotionally charged topic could be the hardest thing they do all week.

Helping your partner feel safer may also help you get what you want. Conversations and projects that are important to you will go better if the avoidant person has a chance to feel safe while engaged. When people's systems are managing threat, their brains are not going to do the complex tasks as well—the tasks that are typically needed for effective collaboration.

We can't read other people's minds when it comes to what is safe for them, but it is almost always possible to read when something isn't right, if we know where to look. For all of us, regardless of attachment style, there is a concept called the *window of tolerance*, which describes the ideal zone of physiological activation that allows a person to function most effectively. When someone shows physical signs that they are outside this zone, either with too-high or too-low arousal, this is usually an indication that their body is interpreting some kind of danger, real or imagined. Since people who form avoidant attachments are unlikely to verbalize their distress, understanding, this concept can be very useful.

Your best chance of success lies in both of you staying in the window of tolerance when having difficult conversations. When having an emotionally charged conversation with someone with avoidant attachment, these tips can help:

- Establish friendly rapport. Don't just assume that your partner knows you mean well. Use touch or eye contact from the beginning to establish it clearly, but in a non-threatening way.
- Timing is everything. It's better to get something done and celebrate a small victory, taking up the rest another time, than to try to do everything in a sitting and push yourself or others beyond their window of tolerance.
- Learn to read your partner's face, eyes, and body language and know when they have had too much. Once you learn to understand someone's window of tolerance, distress cues can be clear. Too-high arousal can look like talking faster or in a more frantic manner, a deer-in-the-headlights look, rapid breathing, or trembling or shaking. Too-low arousal can manifest as dimming of the eyes, appearing numb or vacant, slurred or slow speech, collapsed posture, and getting very cold all of a sudden.

- Be willing to slow down when you see your partner leave the window of tolerance. If possible, establish ahead of time what might provide relief. Some people just need a friendly smile and a pause before moving forward. Others could use reassurance, like, "You're doing great. We can take our time." Some would welcome having their hand held or another form of contact that feels good.

At this point, you may think, "Hey, this is a lot of work!" You would be right. People sometimes require going the extra mile. At the same time, with experience and practice, it does get easier. Doing anything worthwhile takes knowledge and practice, and your relationships are no exception.

Last, don't forget to be aware of *yourself*. Look at the earlier exercise to see how you react to avoidant or distancing behaviors. Are you hurt, angry, critical, resentful, or condemning? If your reaction is strong, you may need to take a step back and take care of yourself. Reach out to offer support only if you have enough for yourself or can feel replenished by giving to the relationship.

CHAPTER 10

COUPLES THERAPY EXERCISES

A Healthy Relationship Makes Life Better

Think, for a moment, of the stress and suffering that you experience when you live with conflict. Thus, your life is improved when you aim for harmony in your relationship.

This exercise is a form of self-diagnosis that will help you to know more specifically what to improve to bring harmony into your relationship.

I encourage you to take the exercises together with your partner, and then use the evaluation to improve.

Note a percentage between 0% and 100% for each of the following aspects (0% being never or little and 100% always or a lot):

- Your ability to speak and participate in exchanges:
- Your ability to listen to each other:
- Your ability to be empathetic (put yourself in the other person's shoes and try to understand their point of view):
- Your ability to support each other through difficulties:
- Your ability to express your gratitude, your love, etc.:
- Your ability to approach the subject of your relationship with the other in order to improve it:

Once you have established a percentage, focus on improving those with the lowest score.

Questions to Identify the Strengths and Weaknesses of Your Relationship

The answers to each of these questions will help you become aware of the positive elements of your relationship for which you can maintain gratitude as well as identify any gaps that you can work on together.

- What do you like most about your relationship?
- What are you missing? What are you not satisfied with?
- What is your degree of intimacy and affection as a couple?
- Does this degree satisfy you?

Having answered those questions, here are some more strategies to help you nurture your desire to be happy in your relationship and to make your love last. The good news is that it is possible. Of course, it involves hard work, it will not always feel like magic, but it is quite possible to develop new skills and be happy together.

Be in Love with Yourself

It is impossible to be happy as a couple if you are not happy with yourself first. Love is first and foremost to be offered to yourself. Fall in love with your own life. Be happy with the person you are. Know yourself and accept yourself as you are. Develop a beautiful intimacy with your inner world. Feel confident, strong, and proud to be who you are. It is a challenge, but it is also fundamental! Learn to savor your own presence.

The more you are rich in your own life and you are bathed in the energy of benevolence towards yourself, the more your love for others will be true and profound. Thus, you can say without hesitation that the love you offer is proportional to the love you have for yourself. Without this first movement of gratitude and tenderness towards yourself, you risk looking for a partner to fill the void or the lack you see in yourself. Two whole people coming together makes for a better relationship than two people looking to fill a void.

Love is a Commitment More than a Feeling

Love in a healthy and sustainable relationship is more than butterflies in the belly and sparks in the eyes. Too often, we have an idyllic vision of romantic love. It is thought that love, at first sight, is the guarantee of a relationship that will last forever. That passion must be maintained at all costs, in total intensity; otherwise, we conclude that love is no more and that a break is inevitable.

True love does not come from a chemical reaction in the brain or hormones gone crazy. It comes from a dedicated effort to appreciate each other even when it feels like the "spark" is no longer there.

True love can pass from the exalted feelings in the beginning to a solid and stable companionship in daily, ordinary life. Investing in a happy and nurturing relationship requires effort, determination, and perseverance.

It is important to remember that love meets one of our basic needs: to feel safe emotionally. Thus, when love is the result of mutual commitment, it becomes very safe. This security allows you and your partner to stand together through the trials of life and know that you each have someone to lean on.

Investing in the Relationship

A committed love is a love where you invest deeply in the relationship. One could compare the relationship to a plant. If we want it to be beautiful and healthy, we must take care of it (water it, put it in the light, repot it occasionally, etc.).

The same goes for relationships. You must maintain it to keep it alive and allow it to grow and evolve. Too often, couples end their relationship because they have not cared for it enough. It is not love that has failed; it is effort. This is a problem of negligence. Like the plant, an unmaintained relationship fades, withers, and eventually dies.

To succeed in your relationships, it is essential to devote time and energy to them. Too easily we take the other person for granted. We get bogged down in the routine and business of life. Our schedule is so full that there is no more room to simply take time to share and be together. This inevitably creates emotional impoverishment and weakens the connection.

Here are some pointers to nourish your relationship:

- Do special activities as a couple at least once a month.
- Work on projects together.
- Take care of each other with small touches, delicacies, and surprises.
- Regularly express your gratitude, your affection, and your commitment to your loved one.

Authentic Communication

Effective communication is an essential key a fulfilling love life. The more you and your lover create an emotional climate of trust and security between yourselves, the more self-revelations will be possible. But it is, among other things, the depth of the exchanges that binds both of you together and encourages intimacy. You can talk about the rain and good weather with your colleagues and friends but aim for something more meaningful with your partner.

This type of sharing imbued with authenticity and depth brings both of you closer together by allowing you to feel solidarity with each other and be connected. This deep connection is certainly one of the main goals of married life—feeling emotionally connected to each other, which you can cherish more than anything.

Some strategies that promote communication:

- Take responsibility for your life.
- Avoid accusing your partner.
- Share your emotions and clearly express your needs. Do not make the other person guess.
- Express empathy and compassion for what your partner tells you.
- Really listen to your partner—do not prepare a response, just listen to hear.
- Avoid taboo subjects. They poison the relationship.

Admire Your Partner

Believe in your partner's potential and support them while they work to implement their dreams. Whether it is 5 or 30 years that you walk together, the goal is the same—to be there for each other.

Maintain a positive view of who your partner is and who they are becoming. This movement of profound complicity allows couples to accompany each other in their quest for happiness and a meaningful existence.

I know the challenge is great. Too easily, you begin to see only what gets on your nerves, but try to never lose sight of the overall picture.

Love is a commitment that requires a lot of investment, maturity, and will. In marital matters, we are all far from experts.

You must make a choice to criticize your partner very rarely and, instead, to regularly acknowledge their accomplishments. Choose to see the glass half full and not half empty, and appreciate your partner.

The "perfect" partner, like the perfect human, does not exist. The life of a couple is a perpetual dance of compromise, adjustments, and letting go.

Happiness comes from making a bouquet with the flowers that we have.

Change Yourself Rather than Changing your Partner

There is no greater or crueler mirror to show us our flaws than a relationship. While the other person may bring out the best in you, they also may inadvertently cause you to notice the worst. This goes both ways—we often do not recognize our flaws until someone else sees them. It is difficult to submit to the vulnerability that comes from being in a relationship and realizing we are not perfect.

Sometimes, we use this vulnerability in our partner to change what we do not like rather than focusing on what we can change about ourselves. Our pride tends to ally itself with our ego to comfortably indulge in denial and blindness.

Obviously, wanting to change another person is a futile wish. You only have power over yourself. It is up to you to do the work of healing and transforming yourself. Relationships can become a wonderful opportunity to heal your own wounds, even if it is terribly scary to go where it hurts.

What if you turned your gaze to yourself rather than blaming the other person? What if you recognized that you could do better for the relationship by focusing on yourself?

Choose Your Arguments Wisely

Let us be realistic—it is inevitable in such an intimate relationship, which affects so many spheres of life, that there will be tensions over the ways of seeing and doing things. Life with another person works to exacerbate the differences. It is utopian to aspire to harmony and perfect agreement in all areas. There will be struggles—but they are not all bad.

So, how do you argue in a healthy way?

- Remember that the other is your lover and not your enemy.
- Work as a team and not as opponents.
- Do not declare war but look for "win-win" solutions.
- Avoid sterile dynamics such as who is wrong and who is right.
- Defuse conflicts before they escalate.
- Avoid words that destroy, such as revenge, hatred, punishment.
- Recognize that your romantic life is a dance for two, not a boxing fight.
- See your differences as an enrichment and not as an obstacle.
- Nourish the bond of secure attachment, even at the heart of tension.

Power is Worth Sharing

One of the major issues in life for two comes from power. We want it. We aspire to it. We hold it. We demand to be seen, heard, recognized, and to take our place in the world—the one that belongs to us by right. We fight to claim our space.

You and your partner exist in and share the same territory. This creates an inevitable power struggle if you do not view the partnership as a joint effort. This can, in some cases, be healthy and balanced, but in some couples, the struggle for power becomes toxic and destructive. The supposed partners of the same team become enemies. They play against each other. When a couple frequently bickers about something as trivial as how to place dishes in the dishwasher, the issue is not the dishes, but the power.

The distribution of power is found in many dimensions of everyday life. The division of tasks is a very sensitive place. It is one of the first sources of conflict for couples. Moreover, several surveys show that couples who have a balanced division of labor are more likely to last in love. It is a question of justice and equity.

PART 3: REWIRING YOUR AVOIDANT, DISMISSIVE, OR FEARFUL ATTACHMENT STYLE

CHAPTER 11

THE NEW SKILLS YOU NEED TO LEARN

Communication Skills in a Love Relationship

In the face of problems that may arise from conflicts in a love relationship, a good communicative ability is perhaps the best antidote for reaching a joint and agreed solution. On the other hand, the best ingredients for cooking this solution are respect, understanding, and kindness to the other person.

It is essential to learn to communicate appropriately, as we sometimes say things out of place or at the least convenient time. This sometimes makes our treatment of the other person inappropriate.

Another problem happens when we try to guess the other person's thoughts or feelings, as we often make mistakes in the conclusions we draw. Besides, we tend to generalize—"You always do the same thing," "You never listen to me," "You're a grandpa," rather than specifying what we do and don't like clearly. But not only that, it is important that the nonverbal conduct coincides with what we are talking about and is not contradictory.

What Aspects Can We Improve When We Communicate in a Love Relationship?

Regarding this nonverbal conduct, some aspects need to be considered. Firstly, in interpersonal communication, it is important to maintain eye contact, as well as to adapt facial expressions to the situation and what we are transmitting. It is important that body posture represents attention toward the other person. And finally, it is recommended that both the volume and tone of voice be quiet and smooth.

Be spontaneous, smile, and don't be afraid to laugh at what you find funny. Don't get caught up in the doubts and uncertainties that surround your mind. Be yourself in any situation without being ashamed of the wonderful person you are.

Don't expect to suffer, don't create monsters in your head, don't choose to live under fear. Living a relationship expecting to suffer is long-term suicide. Let freedom strengthen this relationship.

Don't make up fights for anything. Think carefully about whether this or that is worth fighting for. Ponder and always, always, analyze before you explode. When you fail, apologize. It's beautiful to apologize.

Put yourself in the other's shoes. Imagine if it were with you in the same situation; how would you react? What words would you use to explain yourself? How would you handle all this? Once you have this insight, you are ready to resolve this conflict.

Don't fill overwhelm your partner with messages, but send them message from time to time, saying you miss them. Connect with your love and your partner's love.

Surprises and mysteries are great aphrodisiacs; they keep that flame alive. So, create moments. Schedule a surprise trip. Make a romantic dinner. Buy a gift.

Cultivate habits together, whether it's taking a walk or watching a movie over the weekend. This will create harmony and bring complicity. It will be your moment, and nobody comes in, nobody leaves.

Don't take everything so seriously, laugh at life together. Did that quarrel last Saturday continue to this day? Raise the white flag with a lot of humor.

Be more tolerant of each other's mistakes. We are human beings, and everyone is wrong. Don't want to put an end to every blunder that happens. Evaluate the conditions and see what really suits you; if it really is unbearable, then it is better that it comes to an end, but if it is silly mistakes, forgive.

Don't cancel yourself out for your love. Have your privacy, your date with friends, your time to be alone or alone. Even though you are in the same boat, you have independent lives and those lives must remain unique for the union to strengthen. Acknowledge that we all have problems, sadness; we all have a life. Don't invent crutches; walk with your own legs.

Practice Unconditional Acceptance

Occasionally, we secretly want the other person to change to suit our wishes or standards. That is, we somehow want it to be different than it is. The problem is that this attitude can lead us to feel a lot of frustration, since the other will not always act as we expect, in fact, if he did, he would stop being himself.

Learning to love the other as they are is essential if we want to maintain a relationship. Of course, this does not mean that we have to accept disrespectful behaviors or generate suffering. There are impassable limits.

Now, it is important that we keep in mind that the other person acts in the best way he knows based on his experience—except for in toxic and abusive relationships. As a rule, most of us do not act with bad intentions. Therefore, it is best to try to understand and talk about what we feel uncomfortable with.

Having this in mind helps to nurture an attitude of kindness towards the other, even in the most complicated moments.

Learn to Be With Yourself

When relationship is over, many wonder: what now? Some people are inclined to look for another person; that is, they feel the need to fill that void by initiating another relationship. However, when a relationship ends, the best option is to learn to be with ourselves. In this way, we will avoid falling into another relationship due to dependence.

There are a large number of people unable to lead a life without someone by their side. However romantic it may seem, what lies behind this generated need is a high factor of emotional dependence.

Many are terrified of being with themselves, having no one to hug, listening to their thoughts, or identifying what they want and don't want. There is an inner emptiness that they intend to fill with external affection. In this way it is very difficult to wait for a person who really fits, thus condemning the new relationship to a premature end.

Learn to Be Alone

Life is prettier with love, but it is healthier when we feel good about ourselves. Therefore, to eliminate emotional dependence, it is necessary to learn to be alone. Delve into who you are, and what you really want.

When one loves oneself and does not need others, one is prepared to love in a healthy way.

We would all like to have an ideal partner, people to love. But "need" and "desire" are very different. When we need, it doesn't work. When we have to have someone by our side to feel good, it is very likely that the relationship will not develop in a healthy way.

One must learn to enjoy life without a partner. There are countless things to do, such as discovering and developing our skills, carving out our future, dedicating time to hobbies, making friends with good people, traveling, enjoying the little things. And above all, take care and love as you deserve.

Learn to Deactivate the Ego

We need to understand that the ego is a way of "disconnecting" completely from the axes that move conscious love, the mature love that is offered in freedom and fullness to the other to form a couple, to have a common project of always respecting the personal growth of each one.

If your partner is a skilled artisan of "selfishness," set limits from the beginning and make it very clear that love is not to judge, control, or even fill in the gaps and insecurities of your own through manipulation. To want is not to offer burdens, but inner growth. Fullness.

We need to begin to enunciate to do things as our ego wants and enjoy them as they happen. Our true awareness of love will then wake up; that which stops fighting to give way to the spontaneity of everyday life, to a freedom where there are no attachments and where each partner is the owner of himself, and in turn, part of a common project.

Is it Possible to Change the Attachment Pattern We Learn in Childhood?

We could define attachment as the bond created between two people that makes them want to stay together in space and time. This union is created in the first months of life with the primary caregiver and governs our future relationships. However, is it possible to change the attachment pattern set in childhood?

Psychoanalyst John Bowlby devoted himself to the study of attachment and established that the process begins shortly after birth, but it is not until about eight months that the first attachment bond between the baby and the primary caregiver can be truly considered.

Unsafe preventive attachment: The baby has learned that the power he has to produce reactions in the people around him is very limited. Thus, the most common reaction is that he is not very expressive.

Insecure-ambivalent-resistant attachment: The child has crying episodes in which he has been comforted and others in which he has not received the same attention. This creates uncertainty in facing the world. She feels she has the power to produce an effect on others, but she also "understands" that the effect is unpredictable.

We create a first image of what surrounds us, which we then internalize very deeply. Unless we can learn other patterns later, we understand that this is the way we relate to the people we love.

CHAPTER 12
CHANGE YOUR INTERNAL WORKING MODEL

When it comes to self-work, no one person is the same. What inspires change in one person may not resonate with another. Some of us need therapists, others medication. Some need good friends or supportive parents/mentors/caretakers. Others prefer to go it alone, using books, the internet, or journaling. Some of us need religion or spiritual connection to help us, and others find support groups to be sources of healing. There are so many different ways to "work on yourself," but when you are in the throes of chaos, it can be hard to know where to start. In this chapter, I want to talk about where to start working on yourself, as well as some specific areas to focus on that will help you with your attachment issues.

Starting Points

Chances are you've already started working on yourself. Every time you self-reflect in a journal/blog entry, talk to a friend, read a book, or try to have a real conversation with your partner, you are indirectly working on yourself. To me, the difference between these informal ways of growing and changing, and really working on yourself, is a matter of focus and intention. When I talk about working on yourself in this book, I'm talking about digging deep and sorting out those issues which keep you from being happy and feeling worthy of love.

Five Starting Points for Working on Yourself

If you're ready to start the process, but don't know where to begin, here are some suggestions.

Therapy—Yes, therapy again. Counselors are trained to help you work on yourself! If you have no clue where to start, find a therapist, and they can help you determine what you want to work on and help you do it. One of the most beneficial aspects of going to a therapist is that they can listen and reflect back to your patterns that you can't objectively see. This is why visiting a therapist is a great starting place. You may go in with what you think is the issue, but with their help, discover the real problem that you need to address.

Books, Blogs, YouTube—Self-help books are relatively cheap, easy to get, and can be approached in whatever way is most helpful to you. You can choose based on recommendations or subject matter. You can piece together relevant quotes and ideas for yourself.

Blogs and YouTube channels are other cheap forms of self-help. There are some amazing YouTube channels run by licensed therapists and many well-researched blogs. As with any other form of self-help, be careful of who you choose to listen to. If their advice makes you feel ashamed, guilty, or stupid, move on. Good self-help advice should challenge you, maybe even make you uncomfortable, but should always inspire positive changes.

Support Groups—Interacting with others who struggle with the same issues can be a catalyst for growth and change. There is nothing quite like sitting with people who are in different stages of the journey and learning from them. They can spark ideas for growth and change, keep you accountable, and provide feedback when needed. There are support groups for almost every issue people have, some in person and others online. Find one and see if it helps you.

Write—Begin journaling. Talk about your feelings and problems openly, and themes will begin to emerge. These can be areas of work for you. Another approach is to begin writing your story in narrative form. Write about experiences that shaped you. This will identify areas you might want to explore within yourself. You'll be surprised at the things that stick out as important. Writing your life as a story also helps examine those experiences in different ways, which helps you see patterns more clearly.

Ask a Trusted Source—This must be a person who you trust, and who you know will not lie to you. Someone who is secure and has your best interests at heart. Ask them to honestly tell you what behaviors they've seen you engage in that have caused problems in your life. You may have to find the right wording. You want to ask questions that you are ready to hear the answers to, and that will help you face the truth of situations that you haven't wanted to face. Picking the right person to ask can be tricky. They need to be secure enough to tell you the truth, even if it hurts, but not cruel. However, if you are able to find the right person, they can help open your eyes to some patterns or behaviors you hadn't noticed before.

Areas of Focus for Self-Work

Below are five areas of focus that are common to those of us with anxious attachment systems. I introduce them here in the hope that you can branch out and explore them further. You can easily find resources on these topics. Let's take a look at the topics that will be most helpful to explore on your self-work journey:

Family of Origin

No surprise here folks. You will have to look at your family of origin when doing work on yourself. Many people think they can skip this topic, or they minimize the effect of events that happened to them when they were young because they don't believe it could still affect them. The truth is that our childhoods shaped us and as we can see from attachment theory, we develop most of our attachment patterns in early childhood. We also inherit, genetically, and behaviorally, patterns from our family. To understand ourselves, we have to look at those who shaped us, and those who shaped them. Once you begin to look at your family of origin, you will more fully understand some of your behaviors and where they come from. This is probably the most difficult area of self-work, but an important one, nonetheless. It's not about blaming your parents or opening old wounds. Your goal with family of origin work is to understand how you came to be the way you are and figure out how to go about changing what you want to change.

Inner Child Work

One approach to helping us fill this void as adults is to be to our "inner child" what our caretakers couldn't be for us then. Some people do this on a surface level. They may step in when negative self-talk begins. As an example, you say to yourself, "I'm such an idiot! Why did I call him? I am so stupid and worthless." If you are doing inner child work, you might stop yourself and interrupt as a loving parent and say, "I know you're upset, but you are not stupid. You are very smart; you just got overwhelmed and made a bad choice." It is a way of hearing what we wished we had heard growing up. For more deep-seated issues, people often keep pictures of themselves as children, and talk to themselves to work through the trauma with the support they never received. This is just a glimpse into inner child work. It may feel weird at first, but I do recommend looking into this area to see if it can help you work on some of your issues.

Codependency/ Addiction Issues

Many of us with anxious attachment systems also have codependency or addiction issues. There are volumes written about these two subjects, so I won't spend too much time here. However, I do want to say that sometimes addiction sneaks in ways that we wouldn't expect. Maybe you don't have a drinking or drug problem, but I'll bet you've developed some other kind of addiction that has helped you cope with the feelings you've faced during your life. I recommend reading about addiction in general and doing some self-reflection to determine if you have any areas in your life where you've used an external stimulus to cover for feelings of inadequacy or being unlovable. Be honest and if you discover any specific types of addiction for yourself, look further into them.

Self-Esteem

Many people suffer from a lack of self-esteem, but anxiously attached people even more so. Their issues go a little deeper than just lacking confidence, but nonetheless, it may be helpful for you to look into this topic. Many books out there give you skills and cognitive tools that can help you build that outer confidence, to help you fake it till you make it. We can all use tools that help us feel better about ourselves. If you can identify areas that you excel in, then you will have an area of focus when you are feeling low.

Trauma

The last area of focus is trauma. Trauma is a broad category. It can refer to big traumas, like mental, physical, or sexual abuse, neglect, or death. Trauma can refer to divorce, natural disasters, or war. Trauma can also refer to events that may not seem big to others, but which impacted us enough to change how we related to the world. To truly heal yourself, you have to go back through your life and figure out what these traumatic events were for you, and figure out how to work through them. Forgetting, denying, minimizing, and ignoring only serves to drive the traumatic event into the subconscious, leading to acting out behaviors that, because we don't acknowledge the trauma, seem inexplicable. It can also cause us to stay in a victim role, where we cannot open up and experience the joys in life because we are stuck in the pain. In self-work, you find a way to acknowledge the trauma and integrate the experience, so that you give it the gravity it deserves, but you are able to function in a healthy way as well. There are plenty of resources on trauma, but I recommend a therapist's help for this one, especially if you've experienced one of the "big T" traumas. No matter what, trauma is going to come up in self-work, and it's very important to follow your process for working through it.

The Good News, and the Bad

This process of self-work can take years, and it doesn't have an endpoint. It isn't a mapped-out course that has defined measurable objectives, and there is no date of completion where you will graduate with a degree in happiness. I tell you this because when you start working on yourself, things will get complicated. You will go through periods of numbness and exhaustion, or tears and frustration. If you are really doing the work, you will find there are times of feeling elated and enlightened, followed by doubt and backtracking. You may focus intensely for months, then take a break for a year. Relationships will change. You will feel like you don't know yourself. You will experience a lot of pain in letting go of old coping mechanisms that have kept you "safe." But, as you begin to replace those old habits with healthy new ones, you will find that you are indeed happier. You will feel more capable and less like a victim. You will know that you are making your own decisions and coming to terms with your past, present, and future.

Life may still not turn out as you expected. Your Prince Charming may never come. You will still have issues with co-workers, parents, and siblings. You will still have days where your old habits pop back up, but you will find that you can stop them more quickly and easily. What used to be three months of depression and obsession after a breakup, will turn into a week. What used to be extreme anger and resentment at a partner being late, will turn into disappointment, followed by an acceptance and a decision to continue interacting with that person or not. You will be less afraid of conflict and will speak your mind without fearing how others will react. Everything will seem a little clearer and you will not second guess your thoughts and feelings. You will validate yourself. I believe this is the "secret" of happy and secure people. They aren't perfect, they aren't better or more loveable than you, they just grew up knowing how to believe in themselves. You had to learn it the hard way.

Avoidant Attachment Style and Friendship

Friendship for Dismissive Avoidant Personalities

While the way dismissive avoidants relate to their friends is completely opposite to anxious preoccupied personalities, the result is the same: a lack of close friendships. As we have learned, dismissive avoidants prize themselves on their independence and their perceived belief that they do not need anyone else in order to prosper. This can cause them to be distant and dismissive—something their secure friends will perceive as coldness, disinterest, or even rudeness.

Friendship for Fearful Avoidant Personalities

While we all have versions of ourselves that we put out into the public eye, fearful avoidant personalities are adept at presenting a carefully cultivated persona, or false self when showing themselves to the world. This façade is a defense mechanism to prevent any spontaneous display of emotion and to keep their innermost feelings hidden away.

People who consider themselves friends with a fearful avoidant personality can often find themselves surprised and hurt when distress causes the fearful avoidant's "mask" to fall away. Their friends will then discover that the true personality of the person they had believed themselves close to was little more than a lie.

As a result of this false self, the fearful avoidant often has a group of friends who have been drawn to their personal false self and have little idea who they really are. When their true self is revealed in times of crisis, they may find they have no one who truly understands them—or perhaps even likes them—and consequently, they have no one on whom they can really rely.

Not being able to be vulnerable with friends who are vulnerable with you puts a strain on the relationship, making close friendships a challenge for fearful avoidants. It is important for people with this attachment type to recognize that real intimacy and friendship are based on loyalty and honesty. Pretending to be something you are not—while it can be an effective defense mechanism—will leave you with few friends you can count on in times of trouble.

CHAPTER 13

HOW TO FIND YOUR PARTNER

You may have heard it from friends or co-workers a few times. They talk about how beautiful their relationship is. It's new, and they're excited. Some months later, they begin to say things like, "I'm just not sure he's the one for me." They can't put their fingers on it, but for them, something doesn't work. You begin to think about your relationship. Is he the right person for you?

One of the most important issues to consider when looking for someone you like is how they treat you. Are they kind, compassionate, caring, and respectful? Do they keep the conversation on the floor, or do they stand up?

Next, ensure that your relationship is consistent with your values. Most people conform to the ideals of the person they are dating. They don't know their own principles, so they just try and fit what they're given. Take some time to consider your own beliefs. If you love fun and you are speaking to someone who is severe, it won't match well most of the time.

Make sure you know what you want in a person. Sure, you want them attractive and kind, but what else in a human do you want? Does your job match with what you want? Say you meet a great person, you start dating, and things are going well. The only thing is that they always go to work. They are more out of the city than in the city. Is that something with which you are comfortable? It is essential to know the answer. When you say, "I'm OK, but it's not my dream," then you might need to explain your needs. You could end up raising your children with a partner who is gone quite often if you continue the relationship and end up married.

Similar interests are significant. Now, this doesn't mean that you have to be joined at the hip, but you should enjoy joint activities. If you have different interests, one of you will still sacrifice your happiness. If you're going to be with somebody most of the time, you have to enjoy yourself, and vice versa.

Understand that not every person you meet will be the person you want to marry. It's all right to let someone go and move on. Understand that every person you meet gives you valuable information about what you do and don't want in a partner.

Also understand that you can't be too picky. The above step appears to be a contradiction, but it is indeed an add-on. Nobody, not even you, is perfect. You may have many qualities in a person you want, and they have most, but not all of them. This is all right. Determine which qualities are most important to you, keep them close to your heart and make sure your partner has these features.

All these steps help you to decide whether this partner is right for you. You deserve the best friendship, and there's one for everyone if you're prepared to do the internal work you need to do.

Building Healthy Relationships

Cupid with bow and arrow in hand is often used as a representation of magical love. What can be more romantic than some twist of fate bringing you together with your significant other for a happily-ever-after ending? You may be one of those hopeless romantics who believe in soulmates and "the one," or you may be a believer in making your own destiny.

It doesn't really matter which of the two notions you subscribe to because when it comes right down to it, all healthy relationships require is effort and a willingness to create the reality you want. There is no harm in being romantic or believing that there is a soulmate for everyone. However, you must be willing to do the work to create your own happily-ever-after. The honeymoon phase does not last forever and after it has passed, you will need a lot more than romance to keep your relationship healthy.

Healthy and happy relationships are built on commitment, finding freedom in that commitment and awareness. Most people think of commitment as the ball and chain that signals an end to their freedom. Actually, this assumption is quite far off the mark. In a healthy relationship, commitment signals freedom. Freedom to be yourself, freedom to be vulnerable, and the freedom to give in to your innermost desires.

If your relationship feels like a ball and chain, then you need to rethink the kind of reality you have created for yourself. Being in a relationship should make you feel like you have found the person you want to share your life with. This should free you from the anxiety of constantly dating or trying to find someone you can connect with. Unfortunately for most people, this reality is forgotten when they get into a relationship.

Ironically when it comes to relationships, those who are in them are trying to get out and those who are outside are trying to get in. This is especially common when you find yourself in a relationship where you feel trapped or like you are no longer free to be yourself. Fortunately, creating a healthy relationship is a skill that can be learned. No matter how many failed relationships you have had, there is nothing standing in the way of you having a successful relationship.

Any relationship that is worth having can be fixed if the two parties in it are willing to do the work. The awareness part of being in a healthy relationship requires that, no matter what is going on in your relationship, you always try to remember why you got together in the first place.

You can get so caught up in the troubles you are experiencing that you forget that the person you are fighting with was once the person you considered "the one." Remember why you fell in love in the first place and resolve to work through your issues. Sometimes it is better to rebuild what you have rather than keep jumping from one relationship to another hoping that the next one will be better.

Open Communication

If you want a healthy relationship, communication has to be one of the first things that you get right. By definition, communication is the transfer of information; this implies letting the other person know what you are thinking or feeling. In a relationship, communication goes beyond just the words that are coming from your mouth. It defines how you connect with your partner and how you understand each other.

If you are with someone and you have no idea what they need or how they are feeling, how would it possible for that relationship to work? It would be well near impossible because you are not on the same page. Communication affects all aspects of your relationship, including intimacy. The more you are aware of each other's needs, the better you will be at fulfilling them.

Overcoming Jealousy

The green-eyed monster can destroy even the strongest of relationships. It breaks down trust and creates tension in the relationship. One partner takes on an offensive role while the other becomes defensive. In this kind of dynamic, both parties are miserable, and the relationship begins to feel like a burden.

Jealousy is, in most cases, driven more by your insecurities than by your partner's actions or behavior. It can lead to people making rash decisions that end up causing more harm to the relationship. Lashing out, avenging and even aggression are just some of the ways in which jealousy manifests.

At some point or other, we all experience jealousy. Sometimes it is founded while in other cases, it can be as a result of an overactive imagination and fear. Whatever the case may be, jealousy becomes a problem when you start giving in to it. Learning to manage your emotions is one of the most effective ways of overcoming jealousy and its effects on your relationship.

Emotional Connection Done Right

How do you ensure that you avoid codependency and that your attachment style is positive? When you are in a relationship, it is possible to get too attached and forget yourself. This happens when you make the other person the center of your universe and neglect your own needs. This kind of over-dependency damages any chance of having a healthy relationship.

On the other hand, you do not want to be emotionally unavailable. People who are afraid of deep emotional connections tend to be closed off and detached. This again makes it impossible to have a healthy relationship. The trick to a healthy emotional connection is finding the fine line between becoming overly dependent and being emotionally detached. This can only happen if you cultivate healthy independence while still maintaining an emotional connection to your partner.

Trust-Building Tips

Never make promises you cannot keep, no matter how much you want to please your partner. When you break them, their trust in you will start to waver.

Do what you say when you say. No matter how little or petty it seems, honor your commitments. Call when you say you will, show up when you promised to, and always stick to your word. No one likes a flaky person and trusting one is almost impossible.

Stop being a people pleaser. Be clear on where you stand on things so that your partner knows what you are feeling and thinking. Learn to say no when you cannot honor a commitment; it is better than saying yes then failing to do it.

Honesty is the best policy. Be truthful; nothing undermines trust faster than lies. Be upfront with your partner and tell them the truth, no matter how difficult it is.

Own up to your mistakes. When you are constantly blame-shifting and scapegoating, it becomes difficult for anyone to trust you. When you have the courage to own up to your mistakes, it tells people that you are not just honest with them but that you are also honest with yourself.

Be consistent. Do not be so unpredictable that your partner has no idea what you would do in any given situation. People trust you more when you are consistent in your behavior and actions. It shows them that you have certain values that you operate within.

CHAPTER 14

HOW TO FEEL GOOD WITHOUT A RELATIONSHIP

Everyone's story is different. You may be someone who needs just one wake up call to spur you into action or your detangling process may be more gradual.

Once you come to this realization, your battle with codependency is halfway won. In the larger scheme of things, it is not the scars from your past that define you, rather it is the lessons you choose to take away from those scars. Do not be ashamed of your past, wear your experiences with pride, and as a sign of just how far you have come.

No journey is ever completely smooth and there are a few universal truths that will help to keep you going. These truths are the tools that you need to carry with you to remind you of just where you are going, what you have freed yourself from, and more importantly, what you need to keep going.

The trick to real and lasting change is to do it in small and manageable doses. Do not overwhelm yourself with long lists of things you need to do or not do. Pick your struggles one at a time and take them apart one by one.

Self-Assertion

If you are a play-along-to-get-along kind of person, then you probably do not like conflict. People who shy away from conflict or having to differ with others prefer to just accept other people's opinions even when they do not agree with them. This is especially true for codependents who are natural people-pleasers.

If you have a problem with self-assertion, you will often find yourself feeling resentful and angry and not have a clue why that is happening. When you constantly suppress your needs in order to accommodate and please other people, sooner or later, the frustration of not having your needs met will start to show.

This frustration will manifest itself in the form of emotional outbursts over petty issues, moodiness, and feelings of resentment toward your partner. None of these feelings are recipes for a good relationship, so it turns out that play-along-to-get-along does not really work in the long term.

The first thing you need to understand is that there is a world of difference between compromising and ignoring your needs. In a compromise situation, you and your partner acknowledge each other's needs and agree to meet halfway. Compromise is a healthy part of any relationship. However, when you ignore your needs, it means you have not made the other party aware of your needs and you simply choose to focus on their needs. This is the classic trait of many codependents who feel the need to accommodate and people-please.

Self-assertion is being able to clearly articulate your needs and let the other person know how you feel. Being assertive is part of open communication in a relationship. It lets your partner know what you expect from them and also what they can expect from you. This kind of communication is crucial in building better relationships.

You cannot blame your partner for not meeting your needs when you have not even communicated to them what those needs are. This means that as you recover from codependence, self-assertion is one of the skills that you need to develop.

The benefits of being assertive:

- It helps you to get things done
- It earns you respect from the other party
- It makes compromise and conflict resolution easy
- It makes you less prone to anxiety and stress

Being assertive is not just better for your relationships, but it also makes you more confident. If you struggle with being self-assertive here are some simple strategies, you can use to become more assertive.

Being Your Own Best Friend

Recovering from codependency is only possible if you are able to establish healthy self-esteem and a sense of self-worth. A person with a low sense of self-worth will naturally seek validation from the other people in their lives.

This is what fosters codependency habits such as enabling, caretaking, and many more. If you are to escape the trap of codependency, the first place you need to look is inward. A healthy self-esteem will solve most of the insecurities and fears that lead to the development of codependency in the first place.

Fears like the fear of rejection and the fear of abandonment are all stoked by low self-esteem. To fight these fears, you need to cultivate a sense of safety and security that is tied to your own self-worth and not to other people. This will free you from the need to seek validation and approval from others.

When it comes to building self-esteem, this is pretty much an inside job that depends on your ability to change your opinion of yourself. This change is only possible if you learn to practice self-empathy and become your own cheerleader.

Consider how you treat your friends. Compliment them, buy them gifts on their birthday, support them when they need you, and help them celebrate their victories. Defend them from other people and feel protective of them. This is completely natural and healthy for a good relationship.

Here are simple tips that will help you practice self-love and being your own best friend:

- Spend time doing the things you love.
- Make time for your passions and the things that make you truly happy. Do not feel guilty about wanting some time to yourself to do something you love.
- Get rid of negative energy.
- Free yourself from people who are always dragging you down and stealing your joy. Be selective about who you allow into your inner circle and life. Be ruthless when it comes to safeguarding your inner peace.
- Focus on the positive.
- Don't be your biggest critic. Focus on the things you love about yourself and accept your flaws as just a normal part of human nature. No one is perfect, and constantly focusing on your weaknesses will only undermine your confidence.
- Take care of your body. Stay healthy and active. A healthy body builds your confidence and self-esteem. Take time to exercise and eat well. You only get one body in this life so take care of it. Avoid over-indulging in unhealthy habits that damage your health in the long run.

- Stay true to your values. Keep your values close at heart and make decisions that are in line with your core values. Your values will help you to make better choices and to avoid following trends and other people's opinions just to please others.

Saying No to Toxic Relationships

Perhaps one of the more challenging aspects of codependent tendencies is the tendency to soak up other people's distress. When you do not have sufficient boundaries to safeguard your emotions, you end up making other people's problems your own. This effectively leads you to a codependent situation where you are unable to separate yourself from the other person.

Such toxic relationships bring out the worst in you because the other person knows exactly what buttons to push to get you to toe the line. You will find yourself often doing things you would otherwise never consider doing just to keep the other person happy. This dysfunction if left unchecked, becomes a self-repeating cycle that takes over your life.

Toxic relationships poison you from the inside out. In extreme cases, they may even drive you to coping mechanisms such as addictions to help you process your unresolved issues. This potential for self-harm is one of the reasons why freeing yourself from codependency requires that you eliminate any toxic relationships from your life.

Whether you are dealing with a narcissist who thrives on attention and being the center of the universe, or with more covert manipulators, the damage to your self-esteem is hard to repair. Toxic people come in many different shapes and forms, and you need to be able to identify them by their characteristics.

Here are some of the warnings signs you need to be on the lookout for if you are to identify toxic people and weed them out:

- They like to control you
- They like to shift blame and never take responsibility for their actions
- They are overly critical and always trying to find fault
- They use threats and intimidation to manipulate you
- They try to gain sympathy by playing
- They are always complaining
- They often use emotional abuse to make you feel worthless

Perhaps the most toxic relationship for a codependent is one with a narcissist. Narcissists have no consideration or interest in other people's feelings or needs. When it comes to empathy and compassion, the narcissist is the polar opposite of the codependent.

Here are the classic signs that point to a narcissistic personality:

- They lack empathy and never try to meet your needs.
- They manipulate you to get what they want.
- They expect you to cater to their every need and whim without question.
- They demand the best of everything.
- They are constantly making you feel inferior.
- They have a compulsive need to be the center of attention.

Knowing Which Walls to Build

When you think of walls, you immediately think of protection and safeguarding something. That is exactly what walls do in your emotional life as well. They keep the good stuff in and safeguard you from the negative. That is why you need to build walls around the things you need to keep protected.

Your values, your self-esteem, your interests, and your goals are some of the things that you need to protect at all costs. When you are in a codependent state, these pieces of you get lost in the relationship as you put all your energy into meeting the needs of the other person. In that case, you get lost in the relationship and lack any sense of self-worth or individuality.

Walls help you to create boundaries that set limits for yourself and the people in your life. These walls say to you and the people in your life that these are things that you will not compromise on. Retaining your values, passions, and interests are important in the journey of recovery from codependency.

Tips for Building Better Boundaries

Identify your Limits

Identify what you want to protect and where essentially your limits are. Decide what you are willing to compromise on and what a deal-breaker is for you. You can base these decisions on your values and the things that are important to you.

Be Assertive

Communicate your boundaries clearly and let the other person know what you expect from them and what they can expect from you. That way, both parties are fully aware of what they are getting into and are fully prepared for it.

Cultivate Self-Awareness

The only way to set good boundaries is to understand yourself first. When you appreciate what your needs are, you can set reasonable boundaries that will help you meet your needs.

Consider Your Unresolved Issues

Only you can know where your triggers and weaknesses are. Set boundaries that will help you cope with these weaknesses and make it easy for you to escape the traps that made you codependent in the first place.

Prioritize Your Needs

Boundaries should be about ensuring that whichever relationship you are getting into, your needs are being met. This means that your primary consideration when setting limits should be your needs and what you want from the relationship.

CHAPTER 15

HEAL YOUR ATTACHMENT WOUNDS

As we have learned throughout this book, without intervention, those of us with an insecure attachment style will go on to relive the negative experiences of their childhood, resulting in strained, stressful, and painful experiences throughout their life. These issues can manifest in romantic relationships, friendships, relationships with family and colleagues, as well as the way we relate to ourselves.

But no matter how deep-seated these attachment wounds are, they can be healed. It is important to believe that secure attachment is possible for everyone. There are many ways in which attachment trauma can be healed, and in this chapter, we will address both self-healing methods and some of the many methods that may be used when working with a therapist.

Self-Directed Healing

Healing becomes possible when we focus on rewiring our brain and creating new experiences of positive emotional connection. In time, these new thought processes will replace the old behavioral patterns that were brought about by our negative childhood experiences.

Let's take a look at some of the ways you can work at healing your attachment wounds:

Allow Yourself to Grieve

The healing process is a process of grieving. When you become aware of the incidents and situations that caused your attachment issues to form, it is likely that you will feel some degree of loss and sadness. This grief will come about with the realization that you suffered neglect as a child, or from the absence of any real emotional connection to your primary caregiver.

Accepting the need for new patterns and getting rid of the old is a grief process. You are mourning both what did happen, and also the safe, secure relationships that *did not* happen. Allow yourself to feel and accept this pain, before releasing it and moving on.

Make Sense of Your Story

If we can understand exactly what the narrative is that is driving our attachment issues, it helps us to see how it is affecting us in our adult lives. It may also make us aware that we are passing down the same narrative and issues to our own children.

These issues may be things we usually associate with the word "trauma" such as bereavement, abuse, or other life-threatening situations. But the reality is that most of us carry around the effects of smaller "traumas"—many of which are unconscious. These can be things like dealing with a parent who was always at work or was too busy dealing with their own emotional issues to really be present when in our company. This trauma could be related to one particular moment, or a series of incidents that took place over time and cumulatively resulted in your attachment style.

The issues that brought about our trauma may not always be obvious, as any emotional abuse we suffered as a child may not be immediately clear. For example, we may have had an outwardly loving and participatory parent who, despite their best intentions, did not offer any true emotional connection or engagement. Often due to their own attachment issues, this parent may have been either available or been unwilling to really understand the workings of their child's mind. This kind of chronic emotional absence can have the same negative effect on a child as more obvious emotional abuse.

By facing and understanding our past traumas, we can change our attachment patterns; in time altering the course of our relationships and our, ultimately, our lives.

Find a Partner with a Secure Attachment Style

Partners with secure attachment styles can be invaluable resources in assisting their loved ones to break out of their negative attachment patterns. Developing a secure relationship with someone who already exhibits a secure attachment style can help increase our self-worth and sense of security, as our new partnership forms an active model for how successful relationships operate. Possibly, those of us with insecure attachment styles have never been part of a secure relationship before, owing to the constant recreation of the negative patterns experienced in childhood.

But entering a healing relationship with a securely attached partner can be a frightening experience for many people suffering from insecure attachment styles. Many insecure people, particularly those with an avoidant attachment style, struggle to open up and connect with others, and the idea that a partner may seek emotional intimacy can be overwhelming.

Some people with insecure attachment styles may believe it is necessary to handle all their issues themselves and never ask for help. Others may believe that sharing their problems is futile, as no one could possibly understand what they are going through. Sharing and opening up might also make them feel weak. And for those with dismissive avoidant or fearful avoidant attachment styles, being alone might be the only thing that makes them feel safe.

But for those of you struggling to connect with a secure partner, understand that cultivating a healthy relationship has the power to repair even the most deep-seated of emotional wounds.

Choose a life of connection; not just with your significant other, but in all relationships. Shift your focus on how you define relationships and realize that all relationships are important. Counter the patterns of disconnect you have previously experienced by actively inviting connection into your life.

Make a plan to live a life of connection and value all your relationships. Remember, as humans, we need a connection to survive. Surrounding ourselves with those we care about gives us security, comfort, inspiration, clarity, and grounding.

Question Your Core Beliefs About Yourself

Remember, those who caused your attachment issues had their own problems. These may have come in the form of addiction, preoccupation, work issues, their own dramas, or marriage issues. Very rarely, if ever, was their behavior a direct reflection on you.

Nonetheless, our attachment issues create a set of negative core beliefs we have about ourselves. We tell ourselves stories about what happened and draw our own, often unconscious conclusions. For example, "Dad was always at work; therefore, I don't matter." Or "Mom never really listened to me, so I must be unlovable." We personalize the events that took place during our childhood and develop deep-seated core beliefs about ourselves that affect our adult life.

These negative beliefs form obstacles when it comes to building relationships. How can we have a successful relationship when we are lugging around the belief that we are unlovable and do not deserve to be in a relationship? How can we have a successful relationship when we don't believe we are good enough or don't believe that we matter?

Successfully healing our attachment wounds requires us to really confront our core beliefs and examine just what it is we feel about ourselves. Most often, these beliefs lead us to have a diminished sense of self-worth.

Confront the Romantic Narrative

Our culture is constantly presenting us with an ideal of what a romantic relationship should look like. We've all seen and heard this story countless times—a couple falls in love at first sight, and they are deliriously happy. They get to know each other more, which leads them to discover that they are each other's soulmates. And of course, they live happily ever after.

But as even those of us with the most secure attachment styles know, the reality of being in a relationship is often far removed from this ideal. Comparing our relationships to this fantasy ideal is unrealistic, immature, and unhealthy, particularly for those of us struggling with negative attachment issues.

In the same way that we must identify and question our core beliefs about ourselves, healing attachment trauma requires us to look at our beliefs regarding what a relationship should look like. Ask yourself how you believe couples "should" meet, interact, grow, share a passion, and otherwise relate. Then ask yourself where this belief has come from. Is it based on the fantasy of the ideal relationship the media presents to us on a regular basis?

If we continue to compare our relationships to the fantasy romantic narrative, we are setting ourselves up for disappointment, as real-life partners will never compare to this ideal.

Strengthen our Self-Compassion

This point ties into the previous two, in which we questioned our core beliefs and our beliefs about the world around us. It calls on us to actively cultivate a greater sense of kindness to ourselves. By doing this, we are not only undoing any negative beliefs we might have about our self-worth, but we are replacing these damaging beliefs with a kinder inner dialogue.

By doing this, we will be able to more easily set boundaries, along with raising our standards and expectations in relationships of all kinds.

A big part of this is teaching ourselves not to accept anything less than a true connection. This can be very difficult for those of us with anxious attachment styles, who have grown up accepting whatever miserable scraps of connection we can manage. People with attachment issues have taught themselves to live with emotionally unavailable, or emotionally demanding partners, often out of the fear that they will never find anyone better. They stay in damaging relationships, or with partners they don't feel connected to, believing that a flawed relationship is better than no relationship at all.

To break out of this pattern, allow yourself to question your relationships and the quality of the love and connection you are receiving. Realign your core belief to accept that you are worthy of true love and connection.

Pay Attention to Your Physical Body

Like all other psychological issues, attachment trauma can manifest itself in our physical body. Some of the physical effects of attachment issues are increased fight or flight response and altering of our genes as infants, which can cause health issues in later life. We have also discussed the correlation between healthy familial relationships and health in later life, and seen how suppressing our feelings can manifest as physical symptoms such as stomach pains.

When you are working at healing your attachment injuries, it is important to pay attention to the way your physical body is feeling. The link between our mind and our body is undeniable, so observing the way you physically respond to these healing activities can provide you with a good gauge as to their effectiveness.

Pay attention to any pain or discomfort you are feeling within your body and any areas in which you might be carrying stress or tension. Listen to your body as you go through the above healing exercises and notice the appearance or disappearance of any pain or discomfort.

Working with a Therapist

While self-directed healing can produce amazing results, sometimes our attachment wounds are simply too deep or too complex for us to manage on our own. This is when it becomes important to enlist the help of a licensed therapist.

A productive therapy session will help clients identify different parts of themselves that they may not have been aware of. A trained therapist will help you understand that your perceived strengths are often covers for underlying hurt and trauma and understand how these issues relate to your everyday behavior and tendencies.

Therapy can help us connect to our inner child—that often scared part of us that needs emotional connection, love, and support. Therapy can teach us to offer kindness and compassion to this inner child instead of responding to our own perceived failures with negative self-talk.

Therapy can also help us to identify the opportunities for secure attachment that exist all around us. In all likelihood, we have a network of caring friends or family—no matter how big or small — that are eager and willing to offer support when necessary. Remember, our survival depends on staying in close contact with those we love. Even the most independent of humans cannot survive alone.

While therapy sessions may incorporate many of the self-healing techniques, there are also a number of different techniques and processes therapists may use in order to get to the root of your attachment injuries.

Let's take a look:

Psychoanalysis Therapy

Psychoanalysis aims to release repressed emotions and experiences, in other words, to make us aware of previous unconscious memories. Although there is some variety in technique from therapist to therapist, this generally involves the patient lying on a couch, unable to see the therapist. They will be asked questions about their day-to-day thoughts and conflicts. This then leads the therapist to ask more probing and confronting questions, along with the analysis of dreams and fantasies, with the ultimate intent of uncovering hidden memories from early life.

Cognitive Behavioral Therapy

Unlike psychoanalysis, cognitive behavioral therapy, or CBT, does not aim to take the patient back in time. Instead, it helps you make sense of what is going on in your head and provides techniques for dealing with seemingly irrational fears and emotions. This is done through the analysis of five different areas in your life; situations, thoughts, emotions, physical feelings and actions, all of which are intrinsically connected. Through in-depth discussion, therapists will help patients identify the core beliefs at the root of their problems and help them replace their damaging inner dialogue with more positive thoughts, implementing behaviors that support these new beliefs.

The Hoffman Process

The Hoffman process, created by Bob Hoffman in 1967, is a guided process of group therapy that aims to uncover the root causes of our attachment issues and injuries. Over an intense week-long retreat, the process teaches participants to trace the root of their negative behavioral patterns and dissolve their damaging beliefs. The process combines a number of techniques, including psychoanalysis and CBT. Participants also engage in journaling, guided meditation, and visualization, with the end goal of cultivating compassion for both themselves, their parents, and others in their lives.

Hypnotherapy

Hypnosis can be a useful technique for uncovering hidden memories and discovering the root cause of our emotional issues. By entering a hypnotic state, patients are more likely to obtain access to deeply buried memories and uncover the underlying causes, or causes, of their attachment issues.

How to Find the Right Therapist

With so many therapists out there, finding the right one for you can seem like a daunting task. In a way, it's a bit like dating—finding someone with whom you resonate, and who you feel truly understands you. While it can be time consuming to find the right therapist, it is well worth putting in the time. Studies have proven that a good relationship with a therapist or counselor can cause the brain to literally rewire itself, leading to real, long-lasting positive changes. So here are a few things to keep in mind when you're trawling through a seemingly endless list of available therapists:

- Start by narrowing down the list. This can be as simple as filtering out those who are not in your vicinity. By taking this small step, it can make the process immediately feel more manageable.
- Read through your list and get an instinctive feeling about each therapist. Learn a little about each of the professionals on your list—their background, their professional views, their life experiences. Rule out any with whom you don't feel as though you resonate or could connect with.
- Develop a vague idea of the approach you want. Do you want to quickly remove the symptoms of your attachment wounds? Or do you want to really understand the causes at the root of your injuries by accessing long-buried memories?
- With your goal in mind, take some time to research a few of the different approaches to healing attachment wounds. Which of these approaches do you feel is right for you?
- Ultimately, successful therapy relies on a strong relationship between the patient and therapist. Many therapists offer a free initial consultation phone call, so be sure to take advantage of this. Even if, after this, you feel as though you

have found the right person to help you work through your issues, you may like to begin with just one or two sessions, to really ensure you have a strong connection with the person you are working with. After all, this is a relationship that has the power to greatly change your life for the better.

CONCLUSION

Attachment is the foundation of emotional health, social relationships, and one's worldview. The potential to form reciprocal relationships will have an effect on the emotional health, security, and safety of the baby, as well as the baby's improvement and destiny of interpersonal relationships.

As we have come to see throughout the course of this book, the issues caused by our attachment style begin very early in life, in the formative years before we can even properly communicate. Even those of us with the most loving of parents can experience attachment issues to some degree.

If you have not done so already, take some time to really analyze your behavioral and thought patterns, particularly in the field of relationships. Ask yourself the questions provided and examine the love personalities presented in the book. Can you see yourself in any of these attachment styles and personalities?

Above all, remember that no matter how many years you have been carrying around your attachment wounds, they are always able to be healed. While the process can be uncomfortable and even painful at times, understand that releasing your attachment issues is among the most valuable things you can do for yourself. It is always possible to make changes, and doing so can allow you to finally find the happiness, love, and security you have been seeking for so long.

People, are creatures of propensity and owing to an intuitive longing to re-create and right the wrongs from our pasts, we tend to hunt for similar sort of partners and end up in a destructive cycle. Without sound connections, we are bound to be burdened with mental health issues like depression. Yet we are not bound to keep bearing the same unavoidable slip-ups, on the grounds that our connection styles are not set in stone.

Attachment can be both a positive and negative thing. As the Buddha says, the roots of suffering are attachment. It is negative in the essence that one can place the fate of their happiness in the hands of another, which means it's outside your control. This should never be the case, come rain or come shine. We should accept that absolutely no one but ourselves is responsible for our happiness and love.

If you are capable of giving others love, then it is possible to love yourself. Yes, you with all the flaws, all the tragedies you've been through, and all the mistakes you have made. Despite all these things, love yourself!

When you comprehend that love and joy springs from inside you and that nobody else is liable for it, you can keep cherishing others; and the dread and the clinging behavior gradually disappears.

Like any other conduct change, when you know about your propensities, and you are happy to put in an effort to transform them, you will undoubtedly have healthier relationships. We may not change our styles by and large, yet we can figure out how to make alterations and not allow them to destroy our present connections.

You have also seen how frank communication is necessary for a relationship to flourish and at the same time, how you need to give your partner a measure of privacy. Find a balance between these two. Continue talking to your partner about your feelings, voice your opinions and thoughts. Don't forget that your partner also has a voice and so he will also convey his own ideas and opinions. When confronted with disagreements, treat him kindly and avoid assuming your partner has hidden motives. He understands that he also makes mistakes and is trying to improve like you are right now.

Learn to let go of the past. Focus on the present and on what lies ahead for the relationship. Realize that your partner is your greatest confidant. Cherish the moments you spend with him and you'll have a great treasure of memories to contemplate in the future.

Safety in a relationship is not to look back at what it was in nostalgia or to what it might be, but to live and accept the current relationship, as it now is.

It's also important to realize that a relationship riddled by anxiety and insecurity doesn't have the greatest outlook. Whilst it's not always doomed to fail, it's not going to be a happy and close relationship; how can it be when your partner is always thinking you're doubting them and you're always reading into things? Being at the mercy of your fears won't make you happy, and if you want to ensure that your fears don't come to fruition, the best thing is to overcome them and simply live in the moment, enjoying your relationship for what it is, in the here and now.

There is no shame in admitting that you need help in this regard, and if you really feel like you have a past problem that is affecting you in the here and now, or you simply can't get past your fears, asking for professional help and assistance is a must-do. There is no failing or weakness attached to this, and it is actually one of the strongest things you can do.

There are many options for help and support but talking to your partner as the first port of call is a great idea. This helps them to understand what is going on inside your head and allows them the chance to help you deal with your problems at the source. In many situations, this is enough. If that doesn't work, there are other options, such as couple's therapy, individual therapy, and self-help methods to help you overcome anxiety. Your doctor may also be able to discuss medications with you if anxiety is a huge issue in your life generally.

Don't let fear win, don't let it derail your life for no good reason at all. Face your fears, overcome them, and look forward to a future free of constant relationship insecurities and anxieties.

Good luck.

Made in the USA
Middletown, DE
29 June 2021